The Five Pillars of Guaranteed Business Success

Why Most Businesses Will Stay Small and What You can do about Yours

The **5** Pillars of Guaranteed Business Success

Why Most Businesses Will Stay Small and What You can do about Yours

Dr Greg Chapman

The Five Pillars of Guaranteed Business Success:
Why most businesses will stay small and what You can do about Yours

By Dr Greg Chapman

www.GregChapman.biz

Published by Empower Business Solutions Pty., Ltd.
Suite 22, 738 Burke Rd., Camberwell, Victoria, 3124, Australia
info@empowersolutions.com.au; http://www.empowersolutions.com.au
ABN 14 108 173 708

Order copies at : www.FivePillarsBusinessSuccess.com

Chapman, Greg
The five pillars of guaranteed business success : why most
businesses will stay small and what you can do about yours.
1st ed.
ISBN 978-0-646-48102-9 (pbk.).
1. Success in business. 2. Small business - Growth. 3.
Small business - Management. 4. Business - Planning. 5.
Business. I. Title.
658.022

Disclaimer
The material contained in this publication is general only and has been prepared without taking into account your objectives, financial situation or needs. Certain assumptions have been made based on the general conditions for a typical user of this information. Such assumptions may or may not prove to be correct. Any forecasts based of this information and these assumptions may not be indicative of future performance which may vary greatly as a result of the foregoing. Accordingly, no representations are made to the accuracy, completeness or reasonableness of the statements, estimates and projections within this publication. Further, no responsibility is taken for omissions, errors or contrary interpretation of the information provided in this publication. Empower Business Solutions and its employees and professional advisors do not guarantee, whether expressly or implied, any results you may or may not get as a result of following our recommendations. This publication is provided on the basis that its recipient will carry out its own independent assessment of the information contained herein with its own advisors and make its own independent decisions on whether to implement the recommendations. Empower Business Solutions and its employees assume no responsibility or liability whatsoever on behalf of the client or reader of these materials.

Adherence to all applicable laws and regulations governing professional licensing, business practices, advertising and all other aspects of doing business in Australia, or any other jurisdictions, is the sole responsibility of the client.

Contents

Part Three: Getting Results

Acknowledgements

This book is the product of many experiences. From the time I was just a cog in someone else's wheel, to the time I was running businesses in the corporate world in the US and UK. All were important influences.

Education has also been important to me. It provided me with a mental toolkit that enabled me to solve the problems that I had to confront, and the willingness to seek advice where gaps in my knowledge existed. Some of my most important educational experiences came from my business coaching clients with whom I have worked over the years. I always told my clients, that I don't have all the answers. They do. It is just that they often don't know the right questions to ask. So as they answered my questions, I learnt.

To everyone in my network, who encouraged me, I also thank. I am pleased to say these are some of the most motivating and dedicated people I have met. They held me accountable to delivering on what I set out to do. Only good friends do that for you. Many also gave freely of their publishing experiences.

I also wish to give special thanks to Ben Angel, Tony Clemenger, Judith Field, Dr Carolyn Polizzotto, Ron Stark and Tony Steven for their advice and support. A special mention also to my wife Helen for her help in the preparation of this book.

And Phil, thanks for "The Push".

Foreword By Tony Steven

CEO Council of Small Business

Running a business is a challenge, it's an emotional, financial and mental merry go round and in the 21st century it has become even harder with red tape, tax and professional standards being so much more complex. However the basics remain the same.

Greg Chapman brings us back to these basics and cuts through to the real source of success, you're own attitude. The Five Pillars of Guaranteed Business Success are fundamental to all business owners and managers and will provide a rock solid foundation required to build your business to the level where you cease to be the underpinning link that holds the whole operation together. This book will give you the opportunity to work on your business, not be captured within it.

Greg gives us two views throughout the text, first he outlines the story of Chris Wilson a fictional character whose journey through business life highlights a believable and very illustrative example of what happens through the different stages of a business' life. We can see the thinking that accompanies the many developments and challengers that face business owners. Secondly Greg takes us through the five foundation stones to business success, these are the Five Pillars.

The Five Pillars are explored in detail and generate ideas as you read them. I recommend strongly that you read with a pen and note book by your side. I took notes all the way through. "Planning", "Marketing", "Management Systems", "People" and "You" are the pillars that underpin your business. The concepts that are presented here make so much sense and bring together all the parts that make up your operation and take you to success.

If you take these concepts and apply them in your business, you will start to head towards the goals you set, attract more customers, add efficiency to you procedures, recruit and develop the right people and become aware that you should become a leader not just a manager.

After reading this book there will be a lot of work implementing the ideas, developing the details and making the concepts a reality but you will be on the right track and have the tools to generate business success.

I congratulate Greg on writing such a succinct book outlining the Five Pillars of business success because the next wave of productivity increases for Australia can be found by lifting the efficiency in the small business sector, thereby making us more competitive in the global market of which we are part. The first step towards this grand goal is a book like this.

I highly recommend it.

TONY STEVEN
CEO
Council of Small Business

Preface

While many business advisers seem to preach doom and gloom for small business survival, based on my research they do not have to be so pessimistic. While there is a high attrition rate in the first few years of a business' life, most do survive this period. A far bigger issue for most small business is not that they fail, but that they stay small. They stay micro-businesses, or Micro-Stayers.

Being a Micro-Stayer leads to its own problems. Disenchantment, and frustration are just the start, but there is another course. There is a small group of businesses that are emerging from the Micro-Stayer cave. This book is about what these Emerging Businesses have discovered, and the steps that any Micro-Stayer can take to join them.

In the *Five Pillars of Guaranteed Business Success*, you will learn why most businesses stay small, and the steps you must take to avoid the Micro-Stayer fate. You will learn how to utilise each of the Five Pillars in your business to enable you to increase your profits, to make it run without you, and to turn it into a saleable asset.

There is, however, one step between the business know-how contained within this book, and success. So *The Five Pillars of Guaranteed Business Success* also reveals what stops most business owners applying this knowledge, and how you can overcome this major obstacle.

The steps contained within this book have already been successfully applied by many small business owners, and I would love to hear how this book has helped you.

May Your Business be as You Plan It

Dr Greg Chapman.

Part One

The Life of a Business

Chapter I

Introduction

A business, like life, is a journey. At different times in your life, and in the life of your business, you will hear the same advice or an idea many times, but you will treat that idea in a totally different way according to your stage of development as a business owner. The idea may be presented in a different way, or maybe you were not ready for it.

Many of the answers to creating a successful business are fairly simple. After all, some of the world's most successful business owners had little education. It is often not about knowledge, although that is important. What is more important is understanding. And until you have certain experiences, you are not ready to understand.

When you start a business, you don't know what you don't know. You may do a business course that shows you how to plan and market, but because you have never done these things before, you don't understand what is critical and how you should implement that advice in your business. There is so much to know, and it is all new. So you have to relearn the lessons. Mostly through the school of trial and error.

A time comes for every business owner who survives the first few years, when the owner recognises that they need objective advice on the next step of their business growth. The options now are many. Some read countless books, like this one. Others do courses. Some use friends, mentors, consultants or coaches to provide them with what they require. The source of the advice sought depends very much on the style of the individual, how much they are prepared to invest in time and money into the future of their business and on how quickly they want results. This brings us to a commodity more important than money in business — Time. You can always make more money, but you can never get back your time. If you only learn one lesson from this book, please make sure you understand the value of your time.

The objective of this book is not to replace any of the other sources of advice, but to help you understand what it is that you don't know that you don't know, and to show you the initial steps on how to address that knowledge gap.

In the first part of this book, we look at the Lifecycle of a Business to understand the central issues at each stage of a business' life. And we will look at the life of one business, Chris Wilson Architects, which is an amalgam of a number of businesses that have either been clients or others I had interviewed about their business. We will look at different stages in the life of this business, and the different turns it may have taken with the right strategies.

As we understand what happens to Chris and his business, we will also understand, why small businesses stay small, and what they need to do to avoid that fate.

The success of a business does not just depend on your knowledge. It also depends on your mindset and attitude. The key difference between a manager and an entrepreneur is vision and passion. As we look at what makes a business successful, we will discuss the Secret of Business Success and the Five Pillars.

As we cover each of the Five Pillars in detail, we will also look at how each Pillar can be implemented into your business. The first Four Pillars of your business success are:

- The Plan
- The Marketing Strategy
- The Business Management System
- The People System

These Four Pillars are the foundation of your Business Know-How. What you need to know to be successful. However, there is one last Pillar, the most important of all. It is YOU, the Owner. After all you can buy knowledge, but it is up to you how, it is implemented.

Before we look at why these are the Five Pillars of Business Success, we will take a look at what causes business failure. And it is always one or more of the following:

- No clear business objectives established
- An unachievable or inadequate profit objective
- No sales and marketing systems
- The business is run tactically (that is day-to-day)
- No staff training programs

By implementing the Four Pillars of Business Know-How, these five reasons for failure can be eliminated. Does that guarantee success? If you implement these Four Pillars, and you are absolutely determined to succeed, which is the focus of the Fifth Pillar, I can guarantee you will!

In order to succeed in business, you must first understand what makes successful businesses work. Successful businesses don't just happen by accident. It is all very deliberate. And they all share these features:

- They have a laser-like sales and profit focus
- They use systems throughout their business
- They sell products and services that people actually want

While this sounds quite soulless, ask yourself:

Why am I in business?

Whether you are a baker, builder or broker, if the answer is not:

"To make a profit"

What you own is not a business, it is a charity.

Now there is absolutely nothing at all wrong with charities, but they have different objectives to businesses. You may strongly feel that you are in business for some higher purpose than profit — to raise funds for a charity, for example. Even so, unless your business makes a profit, you are reducing your ability to contribute to that cause while you are trying to keep your business afloat.

The next question to ask is:

What Business am I in?

Your answer should be:

"The Selling Business"

Nothing happens in business until a sale is made.

Your profit will depend on four things:

- Your available market (potential customers)
- Your ability to create selling opportunities from that market
- Your marketing & sales skills
- Your ability to make profitable sales

For most businesses, there is no lack of market opportunity, but there is a lack of strategy, plan and systems.

The old saying:

Work Smarter, Not Harder

means developing skills in each of these areas which will ultimately enable you to achieve more with less effort. Like the difference between a learner swimmer thrashing around in the water, and the Olympic swimmer who seems to glide effortlessly to the finishing line leaving barely a ripple in the water. The beginner wastes all his energy in making waves. The Olympic swimmer puts all her energy into moving forward.

In an ideal world you would attack all Five Pillars together, but owners usually don't have the time (or patience) to do that. So if you can only do one at a time, understanding which area you should tackle first is essential. And an understanding of the Lifecycle of a business can assist you in determining your priorities.

Action Steps

At the end of each Chapter, recommended Action Steps are provided. As you read through this book, keep a notebook by your side, and write out your own answers, the Actions you will commit to, what benefit they will provide for you, and a completion date.

For this Introduction, this is your Action Step:

1.1 Write out three things you want to learn from this book.

The benefit of doing this is the same for writing down any goal. If you don't write out what it is you want to achieve, your subconscious takes that as a signal that this is not a priority for you. Any time you write out a goal, there will be a connection to your subconscious. This is re-enforced every time you review your goals. Your mind will then be attuned for what it is you are looking for, and you will most likely find it.

By writing down what it is you want to learn from this book, your mind will alert you when the information you require is presented to you. What you are seeking may not be obvious by chapter heading. It may be an example, or a quote. It will be something that connects with you in some way that is personal to you. And unless you are alert to this, you may miss a nugget that presents a golden rule for your business in a way only you understand.

Some of the information presented here you may have heard before. However, it is unlikely that I will present it in the same way. My mission is to present this information in such a way that makes a connection for you and motivates you to action.

So write down what it is you want to learn, so that you will find the nuggets with Your Name on them

---

Chapter 2

Lifecycle of a Business

OR

The Universal Cycles of Business, and Why You Can <u>Never</u> Stop Looking For Growth and Renewal

Chris Wilson had just finished an architecture degree at university. He was full of ideas and enthusiasm. Eighteen years of education was over, and now he was ready to begin his life's work and passion. He'd always had had a fascination with building things, but he soon learnt that what he loved most was the design process rather than the building. He was quite happy to let others do that.

He never went anywhere without a drawing pad. He was always sketching something. Either a street scene or a building that he liked. He would keep his best sketches so he could review them. They were a source of ideas.

During the term holidays Chris worked for architectural firms. He did little more than fetching and carrying, but he could see first hand what architects did. Although he couldn't wait till it was his turn,. Chris had one more thing he had to do, which was to get his practicing certificate. This required more study, but it was a largely practical process, working directly under the supervision of another architect in a medium sized architectural firm. At last he was able to practice, although under direction of an experienced architect, what he had dreamed of for all these years.

After more months, he was able to sit his final exams which, together with a report from his architect supervisor, enabled him to get his practicing certificate. Rather than go out straight on his own, he decided that he would continue to work in the practice for a year or so, just until he felt he was truly competent.

This was a trying period for Chris. He could never be truly creative. He was also being forced to work to deadlines and to make design compromises that he felt reduced the quality of his work. He was also required to attend useless meetings rather than being allowed just to focus on his designs.

The final straw came when Chris' supervisor told him that his designs were not what the client wanted and he was spending too long on each stage. His supervisor said that unless he could be more focused and design to order in the agreed time, there would be no future for him in the firm. Chris gave his notice on the spot, and walked out.

In this chapter we will review the Lifecycle of a Business and the phases all businesses grow through. Even well planned businesses go through these phases, although they may only spend short periods at each step.

As a business owner, it is important for you to understand the cycle so that you can better appreciate the issues for your business. The first step to curing a problem is diagnosis.

These are the phases in the Business Lifecycle. Right now, your business is in one of the following phases.

- Start-Up / Infancy
- Adolescence
- Growing Pains
- Maturity
- Decay

As we cover each phase of the Business Lifecycle, look for the telltale symptoms that indicate the stage of your business.

Before we look at each phase, here's the first point to clearly understand.

Business growth is essential for survival. If your business is not growing, it IS in decline.

All businesses follow a Lifecycle curve like an up-ended bowl (Figure 2.1). The years might be longer for some, and the turnover variable. Where is your business on this curve? At different times, you will have different business needs. When you understand where your business is in its life, you will understand its development needs.

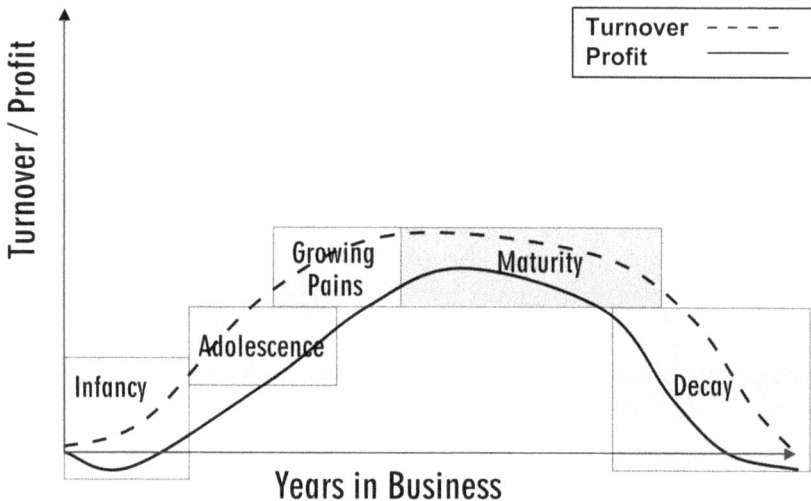

Figure 2.1 Lifecycle of a Business

Start-up and Infancy

Chris was now out on his own with no salary, and just a small amount of savings. It was not going to be easy to get another job, given the way he left the last one, but deep down, Chris knew he didn't want another job. He was sick of doing work just to please his boss. He knew he was good — very good in fact, as he had won a number of prizes in his course. He didn't want second rate supervisors telling how to do his designs.

Chris looked at what had happened as an opportunity. Even a sign that he was ready to go it alone, but where should he start? He could work from home as a freelancer. Find a few clients of his own, and also take in work from other architects that were busy just until he was busy with his own work. He had funds in his account for a few months— surely enough to start his business. How hard could it be? Chris was now excited.

Chris was sharing a flat with his girlfriend Kate, and they had a spare bedroom. He decided to set up office there. Kate was not all that happy with the circumstances, and was a little worried about the finances, although she had a good job, and if necessary, could help pay some of Chris' bills. And Chris was so confident that he would succeed, that she was sure she wouldn't need to dip into her own savings.

Chris made a list of everything he needed to start his business. He would need a business name, a logo, business cards, stationery, architectural supplies, high power graphical drafting system. All of a sudden, it was starting to look expensive, although he could lease the computer equipment and software.

Then it hit him: where was the work going to come from? When he worked at the practice, the clients were just available— they seemed to come to the firm from nowhere. And there seemed to be plenty of them because they were always asking him to work faster. Where was HE going to find them? He didn't have a clue where to look.

With the urgency to get some income, he started ringing friends who were working in other practices to see if they had any extra work. After a lot of calls, and some anxious days waiting for the phone to ring, Joe, an old classmate from university called him back to say he did have something for him, but he was not sure whether he would want to do it or not.

A draftsman at Joes firm had left, and Chris was asked whether he wanted to do some drafting? Chris was initially angry about this, given all the years he had spent to become an architect. He considered a basic drafting job was an insult given his experience.

Chris was starting to get depressed and Kate was asking what was happening, and what was his plan. The truth was — he didn't have a plan. Despite all the calls he'd made, Joe's was the only reply and so Chris took the work as a contractor. He knew it was only going to be short term anyway until Joe's firm could find a new draftsperson.

Chris didn't even know how much he should ask to be paid. He had worked out how much an hour he was earning at his old job, and figured he should be paid more than that as contractor. In the end, he didn't have a choice. Joe's firm were going to pay him at the same rate as their previous draftsman. From their perspective, Chris' qualifications were irrelevant. It was just a drafting job and that was all the work was worth. Chris couldn't think of a way of convincing them to pay him anymore.

Chris kept this up for a number of months, with the odd bit of architectural work that people in other practices thought was too small or beneath them. He was living off the crumbs from other people's tables, and he never knew when he would get that next phone call to say there was more work for him.

There were long gaps between jobs, and the jobs, when they arrived, were low paying, requiring little in the way of the creativity of which he knew he was capable. This was worse than working for his old boss, although he liked his independence, for what that was worth.

His business was going nowhere and Chris knew it. This was making him irritable, which also upset Kate. Chris even thought of swallowing his pride and seeking another job. He knew if he did that, it would be admitting defeat and returning to the situation that he had walked out on a year ago. He still didn't know what he wanted, but he certainly knew he didn't want that!

He saw other solo-architects just a few years older than he, doing pretty well. He wondered what they knew that he didn't. And whether his business would survive long enough for him to learn.

Every business no matter how big, goes through a Start-up phase. Prior to Start-up the focus of the business owner should be to prepare a Business Plan. A detailed plan will ensure that the owner will understand the risks of their new venture and have strategies to manage them, to make sure that their business is viable and has a flying start.

Infancy is characterised by low profitability (or even losses). Turnover is low, and the owner has little true understanding of how much they should be charging. In many cases, they are paying themselves almost nothing, and when you look at the total cost of their being in business, they are actually paying customers to do business with them.

These owners don't have a business, they have a job with overheads, and they have the boss from hell!

Once the business has commenced operations and has moved to infancy, the owner has two big areas of concern:

- Survival and
- How to get more Customers

While the owner is likely to have some technical skill, and is good at providing some service, the biggest issue they have is to find someone to whom they can provide it! Few owners at this stage have any idea of marketing — not even the basics. And it shows. Any business that comes their way is more by good luck than good management, and when the good luck happens, they have no way of replicating it so they don't depend on luck the next time.

Often the owner has no vision, and in many cases has gone into business by accident. Without a vision, the owner has no plan. They have no idea how they will survive. Even the basics like an idea of how much to charge, and how to sell are missing.

In this phase, the most dangerous issue for small business owners is that they don't know what they don't know.

From the owner's perspective the best chance of survival is to bring in more customers. While this is essentially true, it is too often short-sighted, and keeps the owner in a state of perpetual re-activity instead of being pro-active. At this stage, they aren't too fussy about who could be a customer. In fact they would be happy if anyone could be their customer. Anyone with money, or even if they don't have money, they could be a customer!

What they really need are low cost ideas that produce quick results, utilising smart marketing tactics that require only a minimal outlay of funds. While a start-up business owner usually has little in the way of funds, if they can get good, low cost advice, it will quickly pay for itself many times over. The right advice could also prevent a train wreck waiting to happen.

Advice does not have to be expensive. Not having advice when you need it generally is.

Adolescence

Then Chris got a lucky break. After about a year, a friend of Kate's at work wanted to build a house, and Kate persuaded her to let Chris design it for her. This was Chris's first real client. All previous work had come through other practices. He found out from his professional organisation the range that he should charge, and decided that he should go for the low end of the range, because, he didn't think he could charge Kate's friend any more. The way he felt when he got this opportunity, he would have almost done the job for nothing!

This was an exciting time, and Chris put a lot of time into the design. Much more than he would normally. Any change that the client wanted, he was happy to make. Nothing was too much trouble. And the client was delighted. So much so, that a couple of months later, she recommended Chris to someone else. The work started to come. Slowly at first, although as people started to hear about Chris' work, more came. However, it was unpredictable. Things would be so slow at times that he had to go back to doing drafting or basic design for others. Then he would get a couple of jobs at once, and he would be so busy working all hours just to get things done.

Chris was starting to make some money. Still not as much as he was getting in his old job, but in the months he was busy, his pay was definitely more. The business was starting to grow, but he certainly did not feel he was in control. While he still did not know where the next job was going to come from, he was no longer fearful that the business would fold.

Chris was starting to feel good about his business. Kate was also complimenting him on how well he was doing. It was during this time they got married. But they decided to put off their honeymoon until one of Chris' quiet periods.

Chris still could not afford to be fussy about his jobs. Some were better than others. He had some really great clients and some pretty lousy ones as well. The lousy ones seemed to want him to do more work with more changes, and then were slow at paying. On a couple of occasions, they even refused to pay at all. He also had to give one a refund because they were so difficult.

There were lots of highs and lows, although it was certainly better than it was. It was getting easier, and he understood more about getting clients and running a business. Chris was even starting to enjoy his business. The problem remained though, what could he do to stop the lows?

Businesses enter this phase when the owner no longer needs to look over their shoulder all the time. The business is not just surviving, it is growing. Through experience, the owner now knows the basics of business for which no degree could ever prepare them.

The owner now is impatient. Owners ask:

- How can I accelerate my sales growth?
- How can I make my business more efficient?
- How can I make my sales more predictable?
- How can I smooth out the peaks and troughs?

At this stage of the life a business, the owner understands not everyone can be their customer. And even more importantly, they don't want everyone to be their customer!

The question is, how to choose? The answer is to have a Marketing Strategy — NOT just ads that might get the phone to ring. And they are now starting to look at how they can improve the operational aspects of their business. In the past this was not an issue, as they weren't that busy with customers, but it is an issue now!

The business is growing quickly, even if somewhat erratically. Year on year, business is good, although there seems little consistency and predictability of profit. Marketing efforts produce good results, although they are volatile. What is missing is a systematic approach to producing and managing sales.

At this critical phase of the life of a business, the right advice can quickly change what is a roller coaster ride into a ride where the owner, rather than gravity, has control.

<u>Growing Pains</u>

After three years, Chris' business was going from to strength to strength. He didn't seem to have any quiet periods any more. He was ALWAYS busy. He would have thought that this would be fantastic a few years back, but now it is becoming a chore.

He had finally set up an office outside his home. He even hired a draftsman to do some of the more mundane work, and had a bookkeeper to do his books. He would not have survived without this assistance.

Chris was now in a position that he had to turn away some clients. While he had put up his rates, Chris didn't want to put them up any more because he was scared that he would lose clients. Even passing on work was a concern to him, as most of his business was based on referrals, and he did not want to upset past clients who might cease to refer others.

Chris thought about employing another architect, but he was not confident that they would produce work to his standard. He was already spending a lot of time checking the work of the draftsman, and because he was usually busy, the odd mistake was starting to slip through. He just didn't have the time to check his work in the same detail as he did when he was not so busy. Apart from work quality, Chris simply did not have the time to recruit, train and supervise them.

Kate was also getting unhappy about the hours he was working, particularly as she was carrying their first child. She was continually asking him to reduce his workload.

Chris wanted to continue to grow his business, but didn't know how. While he was making more money, his expenses had also gone up. The only way he could see to increase their income was to work longer hours and he just couldn't do that. So his growth rate started to slow down.

It became too difficult to continue to grow even slowly while maintaining the quality he wanted. He could not continue with the hours he was working, so he started to cut down on the number of new clients.

Chris knew that others had faced this challenge, and he also knew that he should get advice to make the changes needed. He attended a few business seminars. The gurus made it look easy to grow, but he knew it wasn't. Growth would require changes that would not be comfortable for him, and with the baby on the way, he couldn't afford either the time or the money. Chris felt it was just not the right time to make any changes.

All businesses reach a stage where they are victims of their success. They don't want any more customers. They are struggling to handle the customers they have. Until this time, inefficiencies in their business could be handled because they had spare capacity. They are now operating flat out. The owner is working extra hours just to cover the gaps. Customer service is starting to suffer. They are making a lot of money, but not that much profit.

In the Growing Pains phase they:

- see a slowdown in growth
- are busy most of the time
- are making mistakes because they are busy
- are working long hours
- are turning some business away
- are spending all their time working IN their business

At this time growth slows. The focus now should be on business systems that will allow the owner to take back control of their business. They need to be able to delegate to others or outsource non-core parts of their business. In short they must leverage their time. Without business systems and procedures, they are unable to do this and maintain quality.

Although important, systems on their own are not enough. The owner also needs to generate reports for every part of their business to ensure that the work they have delegated to staff, or outsourced, is being undertaken in the way they want. Only when reporting is in place, can the owner have confidence that the work done by others meets their standards and they can continue to bring in more people to grow the business.

While they are at this stage, owners also need to develop a marketing strategy that will allow them to have fewer, but more valuable customers. They need to be far more targeted in their marketing. This increases their income and gives them more time to work on their business. This requires a significant re-adjustment in their business operations.

At this point, business owners now know what they don't know. They know what they need to learn. Their choice is between the apparently low cost school of experience, or seeking advice. Those who believe education and advice is expensive, should instead ask: "What is the cost of ignorance?"

The challenge for business owners at this stage is not whether they can afford to get advice; it is actually finding the time to make the changes. They are too busy to spend time to find out how to be more personally effective and efficient!

In this phase of the business lifecycle, owners start to appreciate the value of their time. When they understand its value, they are prepared to pay a price to have more.

Business Maturity

A few years later, after the birth of his second child, Chris had learnt how to be more selective in his choice of clients, and was now operating at a comfortable level, with fewer clients, although with larger projects (and fees).

He had decided to bring a junior architect into his business, and had also appointed a personal assistant. This meant that he could spend more time doing what he was good at, and not be so confined to his business. He had some systems in place now that enabled him to pass some of his work to others.

Chris did not want his business to grow any larger as this would require him to change his role again, and he was uncertain really how to do that. Anyway, he was earning a good income and he was comfortable. Most importantly, he had time to spend with Kate and the boys.

Things were going well. He was building a good reputation in his part of town, and had received recognition for some of his projects in a number of magazines. Word-of-mouth was really starting to work for him so he had to do little marketing.

As Chris had been able to lift his rates again, he was working with better quality clients. His income continued to grow, although much more slowly than before. He would have liked to earn more, but he had basically accepted his more subdued rate of growth because the pace gave him a good lifestyle.

If the truth be known, Chris was a little scared about what he might have to do to continue to grow his business. It was easier to just continue where he was, even if this was going to limit the size of his business. He did continue to attend the odd business seminar, but he could not see how any of the ideas presented would apply to his business. If he brought more architects into his business, he would have to get a lot more clients and he did not have a clue how to do that.

Chris also did not have any idea of how he could control and manage the output and quality of the work of other architects without duplicating their work. He knew he was really a control freak. There were already signs of this with the existing more junior staff he had and did not know how he would manage someone with more experience in the office. To do this, Chris would need to give more responsibility to his staff. When he had tried this in the past, problems had arisen. Chris considered getting an advisor or coach, but apart from the cost, he couldn't see what they could tell him about business that he did not already know. He read lots of books, and while the advice sounded logical for many businesses, he didn't see it as relevant for his particular circumstances.

Chris tried to imagine his business as being bigger. Short of cloning himself, he could not see anything working. He would have liked to double his income, but he couldn't work twice the hours, and he felt he couldn't increase his prices anymore without losing clients. Chris didn't know how he could build a sustainable business with other architects working for him.

As they were comfortable at the moment, Chris was still optimistic. Who knew what opportunities might turn up in the future?

A business in maturity has the following characteristics:

- Stable profitability
- Predictable sales
- Business generally runs smoothly
- Minimal growth
- Owner feels in reasonable control and comfortable
- Owner has run out of ideas to grow the business

Maturity is a very dangerous time for a business. This is the point at which the owner is comfortable with their achievements. Their business is running smoothly. While sales have started to plateau, their profits may still increase for a while, because they are still getting better at doing what they do.

The owner has decided that their business is at the right size, they don't want it to grow larger. The owner is in their comfort zone. They see opportunities to increase their profits incrementally, but they see no need to make significant changes in their business.

The reason this is a dangerous time is that the owner has taken their foot off the accelerator, and the business is starting to coast. You can never coast in business.

In business, the only time you are coasting is when you are going downhill.

When you are coasting, you are consuming the energy and marketing capital you created in the early years. For businesses depending on Word-of-Mouth, this is a wasting asset and requires continual nurturing. People move away. Their circumstances change or they may be captured by a competitor who has a better service.

The success of your business is dependent on constant renewal. This involves developing new products and services, finding new customers, and new ways of delivering your service. If you don't invest in constantly rejuvenating your business, your business will be in decline. At first it might still appear to grow (from the momentum of earlier efforts). After a time, the sales start to plateau. You start to lose some of your older customers and it becomes more difficult to get new customers.

In your sector, some seem to survive and prosper. What have they done? They have made a commitment to make their business survive. This does not necessarily mean to grow. However, if they do nothing they would decline. They are looking at ways of keeping their business fresh and replenishing their assets.

Businesses at this stage require a total review of their strategy. Where do they want to be in five years? They require a commitment to change their business. Their business has plateaued because the strategies they have employed so far, have exhausted their potential. To continue to grow, new strategies will be needed. Potentially there may be a need to change the business model. The owner will most definitely need to change the way they work.

Change is difficult for most people. By all measures, Chris Wilson has a pretty successful business. He has come a long way, but his business will not continue to grow unless he makes changes. There is a risk to change. It may not work. So it is safer to change nothing. The alternative though is:

If you change nothing, nothing changes.

Chris is waiting for something fortuitous to happen to change his business. That is, he is leaving things to chance. Chris can either make the choices for himself, or leave it in the hands of fate. Who do you think has Chris' interests more at heart?

Business Decay

Chris' business had been running for almost twenty years. Most of his work now was for the same handful of clients. They were good clients, friends really. He did not get many new clients. He did a bit of advertising which mainly produced enquiries from younger people who did not like his ideas and were resistant to the fees he wanted to charge.

His team had shrunk. His junior architect had left years ago. He had thought of replacing her, but as he wasn't getting much new business, he had decided to continue with just his draftsman and his office assistant who was now only coming in a couple of days a week.

Over the past few years, even some of his regulars had not come back to him for their new projects. When he called them, they had either retired or had started using someone else. They told him they were doing projects that they felt were really outside his area of expertise, or they wanted to try different approaches and to try something new.

His income had been gradually declining for sometime. He had even gone back to doing work for architects who were busy. Whatever marketing Chris did was not producing the type of clients he wanted. While he had a good reputation, and even had won a couple of awards, there was less interest in the area in which he specialised as the architectural styles had changed.

While Chris had done some courses to develop his capability in these new styles, he found he was being left behind by the younger architects who seemed to be much more enthusiastic about the new techniques, and they appeared shameless to him in their marketing. Chris knew he produced better work than his younger competitors, but he struggled to convince others that this was true.

Chris and Kate's boys were now in secondary school and the fees were becoming increasingly expensive each year. Their other living expenses had also increased. When combined with the reduction in income, this was causing some problems at home. Kate had gone back to work and had a good job, and was at Chris for him to consider a job, or at least more contract work.

To save money, Chris moved out of his office and into an office he set up in their family home. While it was certainly bigger than the home office he started with in their first flat, he felt this was an acknowledgement that the business was not going so well. His draftsman also worked from his own home, and while not as convenient, it still worked. Chris did notice that there were more problems than they had in the past. Over time, the draftsman became more and more difficult to deal with, until one day, he got an email from him to say, he was quitting and was going to work for another architect.

So now Chris was doing his own drafting. As he was not too busy, he could do that. Chris thought that this was probably for the best because it allowed him to save some money.

Chris considered the future of his business. He was far too young to retire, and there was no way he wanted to go and work for someone else. One of his colleagues mentioned there were teaching opportunities available in an architecture college. After contacting the college, they accepted him as a part-time teacher. It did not pay as well as working for clients, but then he really did not have that many clients.

Chris' business continued with his dwindling group of clients, the contract work he did for other architects, and the college teaching. He didn't have too much in the way of costs anymore. He did most things himself. So while his business had shrunk considerably, his income had not declined too much because he had reduced his overheads.

On the bright side, he became a home dad that allowed him to be with the boys when they came home from school, although it did upset him to know that his was no longer the main income in the home. Kate was not overly concerned as she was doing well at work, and Chris was doing a good job looking after the home.

While Chris enjoyed these benefits, he realised, he really no longer owned a business, just a job with overheads.

Businesses start to decay while they still appear to be on plateau. At some point, significant and consistent falls in sales start to occur due to the owner ceasing to invest in the renewal of their business. The business starts to lay off staff and reduce their services, until they only have a few customers and staff remaining. The owner may even continue for some time while making losses, out of habit, and perhaps, pride. They may start to look for someone to buy their business, but there is nothing to sell. They ARE their business.

The owner starts to blame the economy, the government, imports, staff, even customers. Turnaround at this point is rare. Although not impossible. Business Coaching can help. Unfortunately the type of changes necessary are radical, and can be costly. Such changes require a commitment that most owners at this stage no longer have. After all, if you believe someone else is to blame, you also believe that its up to someone else to do something, not you. So all their efforts are focused on the impossible task of making everyone else change, rather than the simpler, if not easy task of changing themselves.

In Chris' case, he was relying on a few regular clients who gradually drifted away from his business. He had also put no effort into generating new business. He had become complacent in the maturity phase of the business. When he started to look for new business, he found that clients didn't want what he offered, and he did not like what his successful competitors were doing. In short, his market had moved on without him.

Survival of Chris' business at this stage would have required large changes by him and an acceptance that he would have to totally remake his services. He would need to be more appealing to the marketplace and to actively market himself in a way that would probably make him fell very uncomfortable. Even so, his lifestyle was such that he felt there was no need to put himself into personal discomfort to revive his business.

In other words, the survival of his business was not as important to him as his own personal comfort, and thus its fate was sealed.

Action Steps

2.1 Review each of the Business Lifecycle Phases in this chapter. Determine in which phase your business currently resides.

2.2 Write out the specific characteristics of the phase that describes your business.

2.3 Write out the key factors that need to be addressed for your business in its current phase.

Chapter 3

At the Moment of Truth

As a business starts to mature, it reaches a critical point where the owner must decide whether to move outside their comfort zone. Their choice is to stay within it and be lured into Maturity and all its dangers, or to move their business to their next level in size and profitability.

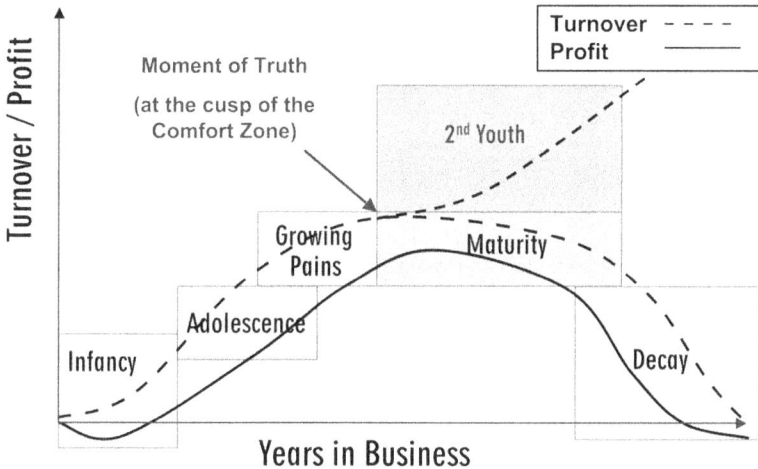

Figure 3.1 A Business at the Moment of Truth

There are two more phases beyond the Comfort Zone (Figure 3.1):

- The Moment of Truth
- Second Youth

Chris' business did not have to take the path described earlier. If we turn back the clock to Chris' Moment of Truth as his business approached Maturity, we can see what might have been.

The Moment of Truth

Chris recognised that his business on its current trajectory was unsustainable. Something was going to give. He could not keep up the pace. Either he was going to have change the way his business was operating, or he would have to scale it back. Either course had its risks.

Then he remembered his original vision for his business. He wanted it to be the premier boutique architecture business in his state. He wanted his to be the architecture business that others came to when they wanted to have a design that would make them stand out and be part of their brand. He then worked out an income, which was three times what he was currently earning within three years. He then wrote out life objectives that he wanted. Chris would create a business that would run largely independently of himself. He wanted a business that he would only have to spend four days a week to maintain, and where he could be spending three months a year away from the business with Kate and the boys, as well as dabbling in other projects that attracted his interest.

There was no way that Chris could achieve these goals doing what he was currently doing. He knew he had to make big changes. He would need to change his business model. He would have to change his customer focus and get deeply into developing a marketing strategy. He would need to either develop his staff, or find staff or other support with other talents to deliver on his vision.

There was also one final challenge. It was the toughest of them all. He had to change himself. He did not have all the answers, but he did have the vision and the determination. While this would take him right out of his comfort zone, his vision was more important to him that his own personal comfort. He would have to learn new ideas, and change the way he worked. Chris also knew if he didn't, the future he could see for his business was not too pretty. He was prepared to make the sacrifice that was necessary to avoid that fate.

This was a Moment of Truth for his business.

Once a business has overcome its Growing Pains, and started to implement systems that take out some of the stress, the business owner reaches a zone of comfort. Their business is running smoothly, and is generating reasonable profit.

They have reached the cusp of their comfort zone, and a Moment of Truth. They can continue as they are ("My business is just the right size for me, I don't want it to grow any larger"), or they may choose, after consolidating their business, to take their business to the next level in size and profitability.

If they choose to "keep things as they are", they move into the so called Maturity phase of their business which has its own risks.

When seeking a Second Youth for their business, significant changes in strategy are required. Although they have achieved much just in reaching this stage, the business has started to plateau and different approaches and skills become necessary. What has worked in the past, will only deliver more of the same, at best.

At this stage, the owner is looking for advice in driving their business forward. The plateau has become a ceiling.

The areas of focus for owners at the Moment of Truth are:

- the development of a new marketing strategy that will refocus their business, and
- management systems that enable the business to run without the owner, an essential step for an exit strategy.

At the Moment of Truth, business coaching for skill development in all aspects of business, but with a particular focus on business strategy and management systems provides the right solution. Now the owner understands the business fundamentals and wants to learn how the businesses they admire have succeeded.

At the Moment of Truth, business strategy is more important than at any other time of a business' life, apart from business start-up.

Few business owners understand strategy. It's not taught at school, only in advanced business courses at university. And even then, you don't become expert, unless you have personally used it in business yourself.

Getting access to the right level of advice is critical for a business seeking to go to the next level. It can be expensive, although there are alternatives. However, if you are serious about your business, good advice will be an investment with a high rate of return, but advice that is not acted upon, no matter how brilliant, is always expensive. So seeking advice must be coupled with a strong commitment to objectives and action.

Second Youth

Chris decided he could not do all this on his own. He had taken his business a long way, but his architectural skills were not enough to transform his business. He had brought in experts to his business before. He had hired someone to do some advertising, and a website designer, both of whom had paid for themselves many times over. His accountant of course had saved him thousands on his tax. Why not also a business coach? This would be a lot more challenging because they would work right at the heart of his business. Even more so than the accountant, a coach would have permission in a way no one else had, to question Chris' fundamental assumptions and make him feel particularly uncomfortable. And he would pay for this? Yes he would.

Chris hired a coach. It was all this and more. The coach showed him things that he never understood before. He explained why different strategies that others were using were working. He referred to non–architectural businesses as well which was particularly enlightening. When Chris said why he couldn't do something, the coach challenged this and then explained why he should.

As Chris was uncertain, even after the coach explained to him what he should do, he implemented things slowly. Not everything worked, but as he was testing all the time, the things that didn't work were corrected at little cost, however, the things that did work made huge differences in his business.

Firstly he started to create systems in his business. Anything he could, he gave to others to do. While this created some extra cost, it also created time for him to work on his business. Then he looked at whom he was doing business. He realised that he was spending a lot of time with low value clients.

Letting go of low value clients was tough. He felt he was losing income, but he realised, after his coach had showed him, he was only losing profitless turnover.

The next step was creating a strategy for high value clients. This was a little harder, and with some systematic analysis (he had the time for this now as he had delegated non-specialist work and was not spending time on low value clients) he understood who were his best buyers. His coach was also able to show him how he could lift his prices for the best buyers. When they understood the value of his services, there was no complaint.

So now, he had others doing most of his technical work. Chris was only dealing with his best buyers who were prepared to pay his higher prices. He had brought in other architects who had to follow his systems. He had a reporting process so he could ensure quality and efficiency, and he had created a marketing strategy that attracted only the clients with whom he wanted to work.

The biggest change of all was in himself. He had a totally different outlook for his business. Everyone noticed it. His clients noticed it. This enabled Chris to go after the bigger clients and charge larger fees. His staff noticed it. They were more enthusiastic about his business, seeing opportunities for their own personal growth within his business. Kate also noticed it. Chris was more enthusiastic about everything!

Chris now understood what he did not know when he worked for an architectural firm when he first graduated. He was not successful there because he was doing the designs that he wanted, and not the designs that the clients had wanted. He was also operating outside the systems of the business. They had agreed to provide a particular service at a particular price for a client. He wanted to provide a service that suited his ego, and did not meet the needs of the business. If one of his architects acted in the way he had back then, they would not stay with his firm for long.

This did not mean that clients would not get the most innovative designs. But Chris did not want to be in a situation that a large amount of effort was spent designing something either the client did not want or his business could not afford.

Chris' business now appeared to have no real limits to its growth. He found most of his competitors did not know what he now knew. He was on track with his vision. He had no desire to conquer the world, but he knew how big he wanted to grow, and what he had to do to get there. He had a clear plan to deliver his vision. He also had no doubt he would achieve it.

For business owners who have decided to continue to grow and acted to obtain the knowledge to break through the ceiling, their business achieves a Second Youth. This is an exciting time for any business. Profits start to soar. But the owner is now playing in a whole new league.

Major industry players will start to notice the emergence of a new competitor, and may start to take market action. The investment is now at a higher level, and there are more stakeholders in the business. The owner in this phase is also aware the business cycle will repeat itself as the Second Youth gives way to new Growing Pains and approaches a higher Moment of Truth.

Owners in their Second Youth don't claim to know everything, but they now know what they don't know. They know the importance and value of advice which could range from mentoring to specialist advice as their business expands into new areas. As the value of their business grows, so does the value of what is at stake. The need to protect this investment becomes critical.

These business owners now have a strategic focus based on their vision. As they are passionate about their vision, they find ways to overcome the obstacles. Their plan integrates their external marketing objectives with their service delivery and business growth plans. Where they have gaps in capability or knowledge, they go out and fill them. As they understand the value of their objectives and their time, this is never an issue.

There is never a shortage of expertise, but determination and commitment are rare commodities. If you have the latter, you can afford to pay for the former.

Businesses at this phase become Saleable Assets. The business is no longer dependent on the owner. The two things that business buyers want most, and will pay for, are a list of customers who will not leave when the owner does, and an operations manual that will guarantee that.

When we discuss the Five Pillars in the rest of this book, you will see how to achieve this, step-by-step, with your business.

Action Steps

3.1 Write out the issues that you would have to face for your Moment of Truth in your business

---

Chapter 4

A Reality Check

While it is important to understand the cycles of business, it is also important to understand the reality of small business. If you know where your business is in its lifecycle, and the reality of how businesses progress in the marketplace, you will understand the commitment you will need to make to build a business that achieves your goals.

Where are most businesses? The recent Bureau of Statistics (ABS) data gives us some idea where businesses are, even though they do not undertake the same type of Lifecycle analysis as in this book.

They report that 42% of the businesses started in 2003/04 had not survived 3 years later, an average failure rate of start-ups of 17%. Small business failure is a significant issue, with few support mechanisms available after the business starts. This can have a big impact on suppliers, customers and staff, not to mention the owners themselves. Fortunately, the average failure rate of existing small businesses with employees is much lower than this, at around 5%. This also means that those that survive the first few years stay around quite a while. The issue then becomes the ability to grow.

In spite of these statistics, small business is the backbone of our economy. The ABS also reports that half of the private sector workforce is employed in businesses with less than 20 employees and that 30% of the nation's wealth is created by this sector.

As we have already seen, as small businesses go through their lifecycle, their needs vary according to their maturity, with different challenges at different times. Wherever they are, there are two basic needs for the small business owner:

- finding more customers, and
- putting in place business systems

When businesses achieve these goals, it frees the owners up from the day-to-day operations to create a Saleable Asset. The owners are then able to get their lives back and spend more time with their families, and enjoy life. If they are unable to achieve these goals, their business will not grow.

The ABS reports that the average annual growth in the number of active, employing small businesses in the 3 years from June 03 as 9%. This incredible statistic hides an even more astonishing one. That is, fuelling this growth are what is somewhat dismissively referred to as, micro-businesses. These are defined as businesses with less than 5 employees. This sector has had an average net growth of 11% over the same period and makes up 61% of all businesses.

What is happening here? A bubble is forming in the number of businesses with fewer than 5 employees. While there were exits (failures) and transfers (promotions) to larger categories, this sector is growing faster than any other. Most micro businesses seem to be trapped within the bubble, with only a few emerging. The numbers look like this:

- New Micro-businesses each Year: 18%
- Annual Micro-business Failure Rate: 5%
- Net Annual Micro-business Growth Rate: 11%
- Micro-businesses Emerging from the Bubble: 2%

Within the group defined as micro-business, there are two other sub-groups:

- Emerging Businesses
- Micro-Stayers

Emerging Businesses differentiate themselves from all the other micro-businesses as the movers and action takers. The Emerging Businesses are leaving their fellow micro-businesses behind. Only 2% of micro-businesses escape the bubble.

Those micro-businesses that don't emerge from the bubble, but still survive, I define as the Micro-Stayers. There are a number of reasons that businesses may stay in this group. It could be a lifestyle choice. Work — Life balance is becoming more and more important to many people. It may be because they don't have the knowledge to take their business to the next level, and become frustrated Micro-Stayers. Or they may have progressed from frustrated to resigned Micro-Stayers and have adjusted lifestyle and ambition in recognition of this.

The Emerging Businesses, on the other hand, retain their ambition, and where they have found they are lacking in skill or knowledge, have sought out advice. No-one knows it all, and everyone at some point requires help. This may be in the form of education through a course or reading, or it may be with a mentor or a professional advisor or coach. The choice here is a matter of personal style, and how quickly the owners want to achieve their ambitions. However, as you see from the statistics, very few people know this and do it!

To become an Emerging Business just requires a determination to do so. The alternative is to remain a Micro-Stayer within the micro-bubble. This can be as a result of choice or by the lack of determination to emerge.

The determination to become an Emerging Business, on its own, is still not enough to make your business a guaranteed success. There is a toolkit that is also required. A toolkit I have called: The Five Pillars. Once you have this toolkit and understand how to use it, your determination will guarantee your success.

Action Steps

What is your choice for your business? Is it to remain a Micro-Stayer?

(While the definition used here was on the basis of employees, similar results also arise when based on income, but direct comparisons of the statistics are difficult.)

4.1 Write out a growth objective. At this stage it may not be quantitative. However, you should be clear whether your objective is to be an Emerging business or a Micro-Stayer. Any answer is acceptable, as long as you commit to it. If your wish is to be a Micro-Stayer, write down how you will re-invest in your business to ensure its survival.

4.2 Write out your reasons for this Emerging Business or Micro-Stayer decision. These are likely to be personal.

Chapter 5

Why Small Businesses Stay Small

The number of businesses that actually fail for financial reasons is not that large, about 6% annually, but many other businesses just disappear. An average of 13% of all businesses operating today (including those without employees) cease trading for multiple reasons every year. Which means that 87% survive! However, as we saw in the Reality Check, almost all of them stay small.

Why do small businesses stay small? Some choose to remain small. But this also puts them at risk, as discussed in the Maturity Phase of the Business Lifecycle chapter. Those that are aware of the risks will continue to prosper as long as they re-invest in their business. The mistake that owners make who choose to stay small, is to believe that time and money do not need to be re-invested and so consume their initial investment in time, money and effort over the years. It is also hard to maintain passion in a venture that doesn't change. Routine leads to complacency which creates risk.

Business owners need to wear three hats in business:

- The Technicians' Hat
- The Managers' Hat
- The Visionary's Hat

Most business owners are technicians in their business. They have created a business built on some technical skill. In Chris Wilson's case, it was his architectural design capability. Their focus is entirely on service delivery. They tend to be perfectionists, and this results in a constant conflict between service level and profitability. So Owners must also be Managers, who always want things quicker, cheaper, and better. They do this by insisting that they deliver their service to a standard — consistently.

As an example of this, consider the most successful fast food chain in the world, McDonalds. I think you would agree, however, that they don't produce the best burgers in the world. Out of ten, you might score their burgers as a six. They are just acceptable, but always a six wherever you go in the world. McDonalds have defined a service level that fits exactly with their strategy of being able to offer a low priced meal assembled by low skill, minimum wage employees. They can do this because of the highly effective management systems they have developed.

Finally, you also have to be the visionary in the business. The visionary is the holder of the future of the business. They are continually seeking opportunities to deliver on their vision. They tend not to be focused on the day-to-day operations of the business. They leave that to their managers. They create the strategy and identify opportunities that will turn their vision into a reality.

So the owner of a small business, who cannot afford three separate roles has to be a little schizophrenic! Getting the balance right is very difficult. However, just being aware of this tension that must exist in all successful businesses often helps owners understand what they must do.

Businesses that involuntarily stay small, the Micro-Stayers, do so for five key reasons (Figure 5.1).

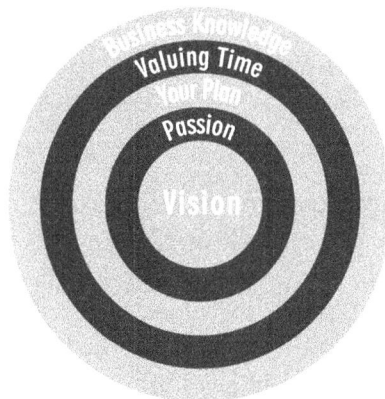

Figure 5.1 Key reasons businesses stay small

1. No Vision for their business. Without a vision, it is not possible to create a plan. The business becomes directionless. Without a vision it is impossible to work out which opportunities to say yes to, and just as importantly, which ones to avoid. Owners without a vision find decision making difficult. They are fashion followers. They expend a lot of time and money trying different things then dropping them when they don't get immediate results.

Without a vision, you cannot have a strategy. Strategy is the lever that lifts you to the next level. A strategy focuses your efforts and resources to where you will get maximum value. A Laser Beam rather than a Light Bulb. Strategy gives you the biggest Bang for your Buck. This is particularly important when you don't have too many bucks.

Chris Wilson, the architect, had no vision. He was just grabbing the opportunities as he saw them. His business did grow, but as soon as he hit the plateau, he had no vision that would drive his business beyond. So it stagnated and finally decayed.

2. No Passion or Commitment. Passion comes from the right vision, and creates the Commitment that will drive you to achieving your goals. If you are passionate about your business, you will be prepared to make the sacrifices in time, money and effort to achieve your goals.

Passion infects others. Your staff, your suppliers, your customers. If you have no passion for your business, why would anyone else around you? When others share your passion, you can turn mountains into molehills.

Commitment will drive you to persevere. Any plan will have flaws, but without commitment, you can be diverted by even the smallest obstacles to achieving your goals.

Lack of success can rob you of your passion and commitment. When nothing seems to work, people give up. Thomas Edison had 10,000 attempts before he invented the light bulb. Now that's commitment!

Chris Wilson, in the end, gave up. Rather than re-invent his business, it was easier for him to allow his business to decay. Staying within his comfort zone was more important to him than the success of his business. If he had the passion and the commitment to make his business succeed, his own personal discomfort would not have been an obstacle to his business goals.

These difficult issues are explored in greater depth in the 5th Pillar chapter.

3. No Goals or Plan. On its own, vision is not enough. Your vision may be that you will be best in town, and to dominate your market, but if you don't set goals and have a plan, your vision will remain a dream, and we all know how often they come true! As you create your goals and plan, you will start identifying opportunities. Many people believe that they don't get the opportunity, but if you don't know what an opportunity looks like, it will pass you by.

> *We are continually faced with a series of great opportunities brilliantly disguised as insoluble problems.* — JW Gardner

If you continue to miss opportunities as they are presented, the chances are that your business will not grow.

In 1953 the graduating class of Yale University (USA) was surveyed as to how many had actually written down their goals & plans for their future. Only 3% had. Twenty years later, the same students were followed up. It was found that the assets of the 3% who had written down their goals and plans exceeded the combined assets of the 97% who had not.

> *Things may come to those who wait, but only the things left by those who hustle.* — Abraham Lincoln

Chris Wilson wanted to increase the size of his business, but had no plan to do so. He had some vague goal of doubling his income, but not a clue on how to do it. He did not even have a plan to get some help. Without a plan he was just reacting to changes in his marketplace and picking up the crumbs that others left behind.

Your Goals and Plans are Your Opportunity Finders.

For example, your goal may be to climb Everest in five years. And your initial plan may be little more than to get fit, and join a mountaineering club. But do you think if you did those basic steps, your path to Everest might become clearer in a year or two?

Plans also create a belief in your success. If you have no plan, how can you realistically believe you can be a success? What creates belief is a good plan backed up by knowledge. If you have both of these, why wouldn't you have the confidence that you would be successful?

When you have a lack of belief, you don't have the confidence in taking risk. If you risk nothing, you will get nothing. Even buying a lottery ticket is accepting a risk, and the odds are atrocious. In business, you are supplying resources, your time and money for a return, but if you don't take any risks at all, nothing will happen.

Man stands for long time with mouth open before roast duck flies in.
— Chinese Saying

Businesses don't take risks if they don't believe they will be successful. That does not mean you should gamble, but it does mean taking calculated risks in accordance with your plan. When you calculate the risks, you are not gambling, and over time, like Thomas Edison inventing the light bulb, the rewards will come.

Having a Plan is the 1st Pillar of Business Success.

4. Owners not Valuing their Time. You only have 24 hours in the day, and how you spend those hours will dictate whether you will be able to achieve your goals. It is not possible to work on your business when you are spending all your time working in it. If you are spending a lot of time doing tasks that you could pay others to do, you will never be able to grow.

Look at the tasks you do in your business. There will be $15/hour jobs, such as sending out form letters and entering data. There will be higher skilled $40/hour jobs such as graphic design and bookkeeping. Then there are $100/hour jobs, such as when you are directly providing a service to your clients. Finally there are the $1000/hour jobs. These are the jobs that will transform your business. Working ON your business jobs. Developing a marketing strategy or creating business systems. Jobs that might add $100,000 to your bottom line. Where are you spending your time?

Most owners don't pay others to do work because they don't have the vision of how their business will be and the belief that their business will be a success. If you know your business will be successful, employing others to undertake work for you is just part of your plan.

If you place a value on your time based on the most profitable things you could be doing, you can pay others to do everything else. But if you try to save money by doing all the $15/hour jobs yourself, that is all your time will ever be worth. We return to this issue in greater detail in the 3rd Pillar chapter.

5. Lack of Business Knowledge. This may be obvious, but it does not mean you have to be an expert at everything. The fundamentals of business knowledge such as the concepts in this book, will enable you to seek out advice and support in those areas in which you are not expert.

While the other four reasons why businesses stay small, do touch on this knowledge, in this fifth reason businesses remain small I refer to such things as Marketing and Business Management Systems which are vital for success.

When you value your time, you will also understand the value of knowledge. After all, the right kind of knowledge can greatly increase the speed at which you reach your goals. If you achieved your two year goals in one year, how much would that be worth to you? How much would you be prepared to invest to attain such knowledge?

Even so, people are concerned about the price of knowledge. You can obtain knowledge in many ways, the most common being to buy a book. Can't afford a book? Go to the library! Courses are fairly low cost. There is a lot of information on the internet, but the free information tends to be disorganised and difficult to find. Individual advice is, of course, more expensive, but it is much more specific to your business and is likely to produce faster results.

> *If you think education is expensive, try ignorance!*
> – Abraham Lincoln

If an owner is not willing to invest in their education, and sees that as a cost instead, they have just resigned themselves to the school of hard knocks. This usually extracts a far higher cost than any of the previously mentioned ways of gaining knowledge. Lack of knowledge creates a ceiling for your business.

Chris Wilson really only dabbled at gaining knowledge, attending the odd seminar, reading some books. He never really believed in his success. When you believe in your success, you will invest in knowledge in the same way that you will invest in others to work in your business for you.

If business owners don't address ALL of these key factors, they are unable to grow beyond a certain level, and the owner becomes frustrated, and ultimately resigned to being a Micro-Stayer. Successfully implementing the Five Pillars and using the tools provided here will ensure that you will address all of these reasons businesses stay small.

Action Steps

5.1 Review each of the 5 Key Factors that cause businesses to become Micro-Stayers. Answer honestly, how many of these factors apply to your business?

5.2. Add to the list of things you want to learn from this book that you have already identified in Action Step 1.1.

Part Two

The Five Pillars

Chapter 6

Pillar One — The Plan

When people think of a Plan for a business, they think of a Business Plan. Even so, almost all small businesses do NOT have a Business Plan. It is no coincidence that as a consequence, 98% become Micro-Stayers. Most business owners believe that Business Plans are an academic exercise, and don't have one.

So many times I have heard: "yes I do have a Business Plan — it's in my head". If I talk to owners later, they tell me that they can't spend any time fixing up their business with new strategies and systems because they have these other problems to fix. Problems such as, someone has just resigned, their suppliers have let them down, they are waiting on some big deal that might happen next month, it's their busiest time of year, it is their slowest time of year (and they have no money). It is so easy to find excuses why we can't spend any time working on our businesses right now, but when this becomes a habit for a business, I know that they are trapped within their business and will not take action until there is a crisis impossible to ignore.

The reason most small business owners don't have a current Business Plan is due to a lack of understanding of their purpose or value. They may have developed one once as they started the business, but as things began to grow, they never looked at the plan again as they were too busy in the day-to-day operations of their business. That is, until something changed. This may have been a change they initiated, or one outside of their control. At that point their business is no longer operating within their control and problems start to emerge. Even then, they will not understand how a Business Plan may have helped avoid the situation in which they now find themselves. When I talk to such owners, the fault always lies somewhere else!

49

If the change is from outside their business, it may be due to a downturn in the economy, or interest rate or exchange rate changes making them uncompetitive, demand decline due to a change in their customers' market, changes in regulation or one of a hundred other things that may occur. Most Business owners say that you can't plan for such events, but good businesses do so continually — and they survive the bad times and prosper in the good. It is all about having sufficient resource capacity and prepared mitigation strategies to cope with such changes.

Change can also be as a result of the business owner's plans. This may be changing their product or service focus, changing their operations or trying to grow their business. In these circumstances, it is no longer business as usual, and if the change is not well planned, doing things the old way may get them into deep trouble. Especially if they have not properly considered the risks involved to all aspects of their business. Many businesses fail just when they look like they have finally made it, when they launch on an ill considered expansion or diversification.

A business owner who is steering a steady course and does not have a Business Plan is merely being negligent in risking exposure of their business and employees to changes in the external environment. A business owner who is making significant changes in their business, particularly seeking to grow it substantially, and who does not have an updated Business Plan for these changes, is being grossly negligent.

So what will a Business Plan do for you and how can you put one together that is not going to cost you an arm and a leg? A good business plan will allow you to:

- Test different scenarios for your business
- Test the robustness of your assumptions
- Manage external risks
- Determine the risks for different courses of action
- Develop mitigation plans for the largest risks

- Develop step-by-step plans for growth or other changes
- Determine resource requirements (human, physical, financial) for different scenarios and at different times
- Synchronise short and long term plans— your budget is the first year of the plan
- Define milestones and Key Performance Indicators (KPI's) so you can measure your progress towards your long term objectives
- Synchronise all other plans in your business — so that there is full alignment of your marketing, operating, staffing and financial plans even when circumstances change
- Roll out of KPI's into all parts of your business, allowing you to develop staff incentive plans truly aligned with your goals

A Business Plan ultimately ensures the Prosperity of Your Business

Why Most Business Plans don't Work

Having just described why you should have a Business Plan, let me tell you why most don't work. Even if small businesses have a plan, most business owners leave it languishing on their bottom shelf, gathering dust!

The dirty little secret of business advisors is this: most business advisors are only interested in selling their time or their 'Business Plan in a Box' but they know that for a Business Plan to be useful, it has to be part of a Business Management System. But this is a much harder proposition for an advisor to sell, particularly to small business owners who are just looking for a quick fix.

So most advisors just sell a quick fix solution. Once owners have prepared their "fill in the blanks" plan, either on their own, or with the consultants help, they expect it to transform their business overnight just by its mere existence. As this does not happen, it ends up on the bottom shelf.

Business Plans do work, but you have to make them work. It is not a one-off exercise. If you buy a 'Business Plan in a Box', you need to understand that you are responsible for maintaining the plan. You also need to satisfy yourself that the product you buy is not just a fill in the blanks product. These plans always end up on the bottom shelf. They don't show you how to do your strategic analysis (which is never a fill in the blanks exercise— no matter what someone tells you).

Business Planning is a real soul searching exercise for the business owner. You have to be brutally honest with yourself. Even if you prepare your plan yourself (without an advisor), get someone else involved to keep you honest! Looking at examples of what others have done can help, but your business will have different strengths and weaknesses and will operate in a different marketplace. And lastly, make sure the off-the-shelf product you choose will show you how to implement your plan into your business.

When a good advisor prepares a Business Plan they will:
- undertake a rigorous (and challenging) review of the strengths & weaknesses of your business
- show you how the plan should be implemented into your business process
- give you at least one review of your performance against your plan six months after the plan has been delivered.

While this will require a larger investment than a 'Business Plan in a Box' and is a harder sell for an advisor, this will ensure that your plan does not end up on the bottom shelf and that your investment is not wasted!

Business Planning is not an easy process. It takes time and commitment. You don't just do it once. This is not what business owners want to hear, and what most advisors won't tell you, because it might cost them a sale. But the rewards from a well implemented Business Plan are worth many times your investment.

Creating Your Goals

The first step in a Business Plan is setting your goals. This is a process of defining specific objectives rather than the vague aspirations that most business owners have in their minds. Unless your goals are specific, it is most unlikely they will ever be achieved.

When creating your goals, start with your vision five years from now. Make it as detailed as possible. For example, answer the following questions:

- What will be my turnover?
- What will be my profit?
- How many sales will this require?
- How many staff will I require to achieve this profit?
- What products/services will I be selling then?
- What other resources will I require?
- Where will I be located?
- Who will be my customers?

Then consider what the goals will be three years from now, and then what they will be this year.

> **Action Steps**
>
> 6.1 Write out your goals in as detailed a form as you can. Describe your business a year from now, 3 years from now, and five years from now.
>
> To assist you in this process, please use the Business Goals Generator Tool provided with this book. Directions for access to this tool are in the Resources section. This tool provides a step by step process in creating short term goals.

Risk Analysis

An integral part of any Business Plan is a risk analysis. This is a stress test for your business for changes within, and outside your control — a "what-if" analysis. Mitigation plans for the largest risks should then be developed to reduce risks to a tolerable level. For example, if you were developing a new product, you might start with market surveys before making a major investment.

Most business failures occur because owners have not undertaken a risk analysis and have not put in place strategies to manage that risk. In this section you will identify the key risks to your business, and put in place a strategy to address those risks. You will also identify opportunities for your business.

The tool used to undertake this analysis is called the SWOT Analysis, which stands for Strengths, Weaknesses, Opportunities and Threats. This analysis is best done with several people, and ideally with someone who can be considered as objective.

Strengths and Weaknesses are generally internal characteristics of your business that may help or hinder you in achieving your goals. Your business might have strong financial resources, which is a strength. Your business might be new, and therefore have unsophisticated systems— a weakness.

List as many strengths and weakness in your business as you can. Then challenge each one — what is the proof that something is a strength or weakness, and what is the benefit or risk in each case?

Financial strength (as demonstrated by your balance sheet) means you can invest in your business, and ride out swings in sales— this is clearly a strength. If your systems are still under development (easy to prove!), this could impact on the quality of your service, which will reduce the amount you can charge, and affect your reputation.

Opportunities and Threats generally arise in the external business environment. An economic downturn would be a threat if you sell consumer luxuries, but an opportunity if you have an insolvency business! Other factors to be considered include, technological, social, and political. Consider also competitors and suppliers. How do each of these factors impact on your business, both positively and negatively? Often, a threat can also be an opportunity if you have a plan to address it in your market niche in a way no one else is.

List as many opportunities and threats that you can for your business. Again, for each there must be a proof, and a benefit or risk.

Action Steps

6.2 Complete your SWOT analysis using the table below. Check that you have been as objective a possible. (If you are being too kind to yourself, the only person you are fooling is you. If you can, get someone independent to do a workshop with you on this part of the Business Plan.)

6.3 For each weakness and threat, come up with a plan to address it. For example, if your weakness is that you are new in the market, you would put in place a marketing strategy to get you noticed. If the threat was technological, you might consider undertaking some research and development for your business. By undertaking this analysis, you are insuring your business.

6.4 For each strength, develop a plan to utilise that strength to reach your goals faster. For example, if you have strong finances, you might buy a market position by merging with another business. For each opportunity you have identified, create a plan to exploit that opportunity. For example, a key competitor might be retiring. What can you do to capture their market share? This analysis will make your business prosper

6.5 List your key business risks, the potential impact on your business, and how you will address each one.

STRENGTHS	WEAKNESSES
OPPORTUNITIES	THREATS

Your Business Plan

Once you have defined your goals, and your market strategy (2nd Pillar), it is possible to develop a step-by-step plan to achieve your business goals. It is essential when you do this that you consider the impact of the changes that will occur to your business through every aspect of your organisation.

As your business grows, there will be supplier impacts, changes in your organisation structure, staff and the need for more effective operating systems — as well as many other changes you need to consider. Businesses, as they grow, often pay too little attention to their systems (the 3rd Pillar). Where organisational redundancy was able to cover for lack of efficiency at lower demand levels, as sales increase, the inefficiency starts to impact on customer service as the slack in your business disappears.

The last step of Your Plan is a cash flow projection for 3-5 years. This is developed from forecasts of your overheads, operating costs, and marketing costs, as well as sales projections. A good Business Plan will do this for more than one scenario.

There is a tension between having goals that will stretch you and realistic goals. When your business is new and you have little in the way of hard evidence of what your sales might be like, be conservative. Undertake a breakeven analysis. That is, how many sales do you need to make just to survive? If this is a large number, this indicates that your business has a high degree of risk. If it is low, you can be far more comfortable in the investment of your resources in this venture.

With a business with a track record, stretch targets are healthy. Even so, behind each target that is significantly higher than your previous history, there must be a clear plan to achieve it. If you are targeting higher sales, what will cause this to happen? More advertising, sales training? It is important to document this as part of your plan.

More detail about business planning can be found in the Resources section where you can find out how to access a comprehensive Business Plan Template. This Template also shows you how to create a budget.

Once you have completed your Business Plan, don't make the mistake that the majority of the minority of business owners who actually prepare a plan make — don't put it in the bottom drawer, never to see the light of day again. Your Business Plan is a living document — to be updated at least annually, and reviewed quarterly. It is there to keep you on track — and to make you accountable to the one person who will not accept excuses — YOU! There is nothing like a *written* promise to yourself that will keep you focused on your goals.

Chris Wilson considered his options. Today, he was turning over around $200,000. He had to pay his draftsman, his assistant, his office costs and other expenses. He was actually taking home about $80,000. He decided he wanted to be able to increase that to $250,000 in three years. He knew he could not do that the way he was currently operating. So he started to do some planning.

He would clearly have to increase his sales to earn his target income, but he could not handle that amount of business by himself. He would have to bring other architects into the business. This brought back his old fear of not being able to maintain quality, and if he brought in new architects, he would also need to get new clients.

Chris now realised that to achieve his goal, he was going to need help as he did not know how to address these issues. This was probably his greatest weakness. His strength, he knew, was his design ability. His clients always raved about his designs. So he had a growing fan club. If he was able to exploit this, it would be a great opportunity for his business. He also knew most of his competitors were not going to leave their comfort zones. Another opportunity for him. His biggest threat was that if he did nothing, he would stay in his comfort zone, and risk the eventual decay of his business.

In reviewing his SWOT analysis, Chris knew in order to address his weaknesses and avoid the risk of the long term decay of his business, he would have to invest in advice. He would hire a coach. While this was not at all cheap, Chris knew that if the coach could show him how to reach his goal, the cost would be repaid many times over.

A coach would show Chris how he could leverage his skills so that his business could grow. Coaching would also show Chris how to find new clients, building on his strengths and the opportunities he knew were there. A coach would also help him with strategies to address the risks, and help him create a plan that he could follow with confidence.

Action Steps

6.6 List the Key Result Areas (KRA's) for your business. These are likely to include your turnover, profit, types of products and services, your customer description (including location), the number of staff and any other descriptor of you business.

6.7 Describe for each of these KRA's, what you business looks like today, and describe it for some point in the future. Use the One Page Business Plan Summary on the next page to record this.

6.8 Describe the actions you will take to move from your position today, to your future position.

6.9 Describe the strategies you will use to achieve your goals in the One Page Business Plan Summary.

6.10 Get your free copy of the full Business Plan Template. For details, see the Resources section at the end of the book.

One Page Business Plan Summary

	Today	Action Plan to Achieve Goal	In 5 Years Time
Key Result Area 1			
Key Result Area 2			
Key Result Area 3			
Key Result Area 4			

Strategy Summary

Strategy 1
Strategy 2
Strategy 3

Chapter 7

Pillar Two – Marketing Strategy

The reason most businesses struggle is because they have no marketing strategy. Most rely on passive word-of-mouth with a little advertising. Sometimes this works, but often it doesn't. These businesses suffer swings in their sales from month to month, and year to year.

This is reactive marketing, with no strategy. This tactical approach is a hand to mouth existence and becomes a daily battle to make sales. You will never have a business that runs without you if you just act tactically and you never create a market position for your business.

Why do you need a Market Strategy? The average consumer receives up to 3,000 commercial messages every day — 50% more than just ten years ago. You must rise above the commercial clutter to attract your customers' attention.

The second major reason a Marketing Strategy is essential is that because of increased competition, the cost to get in front of a buyer has doubled in the last ten years, and when you do meet one, the results are half what they were. As a consequence, it now costs twice as much to get half the result compared with the last decade. Unless you have an effective Marketing Strategy, your business will not be successful. For best results, Marketing Strategy should be developed as part of a Business Plan.

The strategic approach is to create a long range plan to achieve a market position, and to give you an exit strategy. The ultimate objective of Strategic Marketing is:

Every time someone in your Marketplace wants your product or service, they think of you first.

This is called Top of Mind Awareness. When you create this Top of Mind Awareness in your marketplace, you will have created an Ultimate Strategic Position for your business, with every tactical effort now supporting your long term plan and strategy.

Marketing is Not Advertising

Too many business owners believe that marketing their business means just paying for a few ads. What few understand is that Advertising is not the same as Marketing. Many clients have come to me only after they have wasted large sums of money by copying their competitors with "me too" advertising. And the media and advertising agencies love it. When you approach an advertising agency, their mission will be to convince you to spend your entire marketing budget with them, not to help you devise a marketing strategy for your business which will look at all available marketing options, not just advertising.

When developing a marketing strategy for your business, you must consider a number of aspects of your marketplace, before even thinking of your own business. You need to answer the following questions:

- Who are your competitors?
- Who are your customers?
- Can you segment your marketplace and identify a niche?
- How do your customers make a buying decision?
- Who else has customers who could be your customers?

Once you understand your marketplace you should then consider your business. At this point of the marketing process you would ask the following questions:

- What is the ultimate benefit of my products and services for my customers?
- Why should people buy from me?

- What is my offer? (Product / Service / Price / Support / Guarantee etc.)
- How do I define My Marketplace? (Who / What / Where / When and How)

Only once you have answered these questions, should you ask the one that most businesses try to answer first:

- *How will I promote my business?*

When answering this question, consider all the promotional options, not just advertising. Some of the marketing options available to you are:

> *Networking, newsletters, cold calls, special offers, public relations, referrals, joint ventures, trade shows, seminars, workshops, internet marketing, sponsorship, media advertising, yellow pages, direct mail and brochures.*

All of these methods are, in one form or another, lead generation strategies. Some may cost little or no money, just your time, which you must also value. So in all cases you are buying customers, and the bottom line for every one of these tactics is the cost per qualified lead, which is how you decide how to spend your promotional dollar.

When you approach an advertising agency, you must already know how much want to spend on that marketing channel. While they may give you good advice on how to spend your money in their channel, they will not consider alternatives which may be better for your business.

It is also essential to consider whether the selected channel is capable of generating qualified leads at a reasonable price. For example, if your product is upmarket, generating leads from the budget market is of no value to you. There is also false economy in choosing low rating media which often generate no leads at all!

Whichever marketing channel you choose, it is absolutely essential you measure the results from each promotion. Over a period of time, you will learn which ones work best for you. This can be a lengthy experience. Using a marketing advisor can greatly reduce the painful and often costly learning curve, and can save you many thousands of dollars in your marketing costs, and even more importantly, in the opportunity cost of lost time.

Who are Your Customers?

Although this is an obvious question, few owners have really considered the answer in depth, and many would say: "I can help everyone." But not everyone can be your customer. In fact, you would prefer some were not! So create a detailed list of your current customers. Are there some common characteristics such as age, gender, geographic area, income, business type? Describe in as much detail as you can, your ideal customer.

Have you created a niche for yourself? There are many reasons for having a niche.

- A Jack of all trades is usually a Master of none
- People pay more for a specialist
- You become recognised in your niche
- It is a place you can dominate if you are small
- You reduce your competition
- You reduce the time you spend on quoting for work you will only win on price
- You will win more business
- It is easier to promote

Here are some questions to ask to help identify your niche:

- What types of products / services are you good at?
- What types of products / services do you enjoy providing most?

- Which types of products / services do you sell most of?
- Which types of products / services make you most money?

In most businesses, 80% of the value comes from 20% of the customers. These are your Best Buyers. Imagine if you could double or triple the numbers of these buyers? Who are your best buyers?

Action Steps

7.1 Describe your key customer types. Do you have a Niche?

7.2 Who are your Best Buyers? Why are they your Best Buyers?

Your Unique Selling Points

Your objective in defining your Market Strategy development is to truly understand the customers' needs and to understand how you can satisfy them; and in particular what is it that differentiates your service from that of your competitors, and why your competitors' customers should prefer your service.

In this way, you define your Market Position and your Points of Difference or your Unique Selling Points. This strategic analysis will enable you to properly identify your best customers and how you should promote your business to them.

Find, or create Unique Selling Points that appeal to your target customers. This could be that you are the cheapest in your suburb, the fastest delivery, the largest range, etc. Target the customers that most value that particular benefit. When you promote your business to them, they will be more willing to buy from you rather than your competitors.

Too many owners say: "My point of difference is the Quality of my service." But what does this mean? Everyone says that they have a quality service. Have you ever heard anyone say: "Buy from me, my service is is lousy?" Quality is a pre-requisite. Your point of difference must have a clear benefit for your customers. What is the benefit of your "Quality"? If you can't explain it, why do you think your customers will understand and value it?

Only customers within your niche value your Unique Selling Points. And because they are unique, at least in your marketplace, when customers from your niche hear about them, they will buy from you in preference to your competitors who cannot compete on these points. However, when you move outside the niche that values your Unique Selling Points, you can only compete on price.

For example, if you are a mechanic, you may fully detail the car with a hand wash and polish to a showroom finish at the end of the service. This would be highly valued by proud owners of luxury cars. For someone with a low cost mass produced car, they would see this as an unnecessary cost in getting their car serviced.

When you have established your Unique Selling Points, you increase the perceived value of your product, it is no longer a commodity, and you can increase your profit per sale through your pricing. A recent survey showed that price is the fifth ranked reason people buy.

The top five reasons people buy are:

1. Confidence that your product / service will meet their needs
2. Quality of the product / service
3. The level of service that is provided
4. Selection or range of offers
5. Price

Why should someone buy from YOU?

Action Steps

7.3 Describe the benefits of your service to your customers. Examine your competitors. What do they do, and how can you be different (better) than them in your niche?

You can use the SWOT analysis technique (from the last chapter) focused just on your products and services.

7.4 What are your Unique Selling Points?

The Five Profit Drivers

Your Marketing Plan should be developed once you have defined your Marketing Strategy. Having identified your target market, and your Unique Selling Points it is time to develop your offer to your marketplace. This will be built around the identified customer needs of your target market, and your points of difference.

A good Marketing Plan will focus on the Five Profit Drivers:

- Increasing the number of Enquiries
- Increasing the conversion rate of Enquiries to Sales
- Increasing the Average Value per Sale
- Increasing the number of Times a Customers Buys from You
- Increasing the Profit per Sale

	Number of Enquiries	Conversion Factor	Number of Sales	Average Value/Sale	Sales/Year per Customer	Turnover per year	Profit Margin	Gross Profit
	10,000	10%	1,000	$500	2	$1,000,000	25%	$250,000
Improvement Factor	10%	10%		10%	10%		10%	
	11,000	11%	1,210	$550	2.2	$1,464,100	27.5%	$402,628

Figure 7.1 Five Profit Drivers Example

In the example above (Figure 7.1), with 10,000 enquiries, or contacts, there was a 10% conversion factor to sales. With an average sale value of $500, and two sales per customer per year, the annual turnover was one million dollars. If there was a 25% profit margin, there would be $250,000 profit.

Each of the profit drivers can be increased with a focussed effort. In this example, a 10% increase in each of the Profit Drivers was set as the target. In marketing terms, a 10% increase in each area is usually not difficult to achieve. Look at each of the Profit Driver increases in the example above. Few would argue that such increases in each area are not possible. But, if this was achieved across each of the Profit Drivers, a 62% increase in profit would be the result. If the increase was 15%, profits would be doubled.

This is an example of the power of Marketing Leverage. It is not always possible to evenly increase each of the Profit Drivers. In many businesses, there are just one or two profit drivers where the increase is easiest, with increases in the others being more difficult. However, I have yet to see a business that has maximised all Five Profit Drivers.

Action Steps

7.5 Look at your Marketing results over the last year. How many Enquiries did you get? What was the Sales Conversion? What was your Average Value per Sale? How many times per year did the average customer buy from you? What was your Average Margin per Sale? What was your Gross Profit?

If you don't have this information available, I suggest you start collecting it NOW!

7.6 Use the Profit Driver Calculator from the Resources Section to look at the potential for your business. Which Profit Drivers do you believe it will be easiest to increase? Which ones have the greatest scope?

7.7 Set Profit Driver targets for your business.

Increasing Enquiries

What marketing strategy are you going to use to communicate with your customers and entice them to buy? There are really only four types of marketing. All marketing falls into one of the following categories, or is a combination of them:

1. Advertising
2. Public Relations
3. Word of Mouth
4. Cold Calling

These are all different Lead Generation Strategies. Ultimately, they will be compared in their effectiveness by the Cost per Lead for each strategy. While Word-of-Mouth is the most common strategy used by small business, it is a wasting asset. People move away, change suppliers, or just don't need your services anymore. So it is generally not enough on its own. And certainly not in a passive form, waiting for someone to refer you to a friend or colleague.

Generally a business will use a portfolio of these tactics and not rely on any single one. In different industries a different mix of strategies will be used, tailored for their potential customer profile.

Increasing Enquiries, or Lead Generation, for many business owners, is the main focus of their marketing. Successful businesses use a wide mix of the strategic marketing channels, such as: Direct Mail, Customer Education, Advertising, Public Relations, Personal Contact, Company Brochures, Alliances and Online Marketing.

Your Marketing Plan will define the right mix for your Best Buyers, and ensure that each channel supports and is linked in some way to every other channel, and that they all focus on your Unique Selling Points and are targeted towards your identified market.

What this means in practice is that you will use your Unique Selling Points in all your marketing. Your marketing will be primarily focussed towards your best buyers, and each marketing channel will leverage every other channel. For example, all your media advertising will direct people to your website for further information about your business, and your website will be designed to be integral to your sales pipeline.

Action Steps

To determine where to spend your lead generation budget take these steps:

7.8 Monitor the sources of your enquiries.

7.9 Calculate the Cost per Lead by enquiry source.

7.10 Monitor the quality of the leads by enquiry source.

Your Sales Pipeline

There is a large amount of confusion between Marketing and Sales. Too many people hire sales staff without a Marketing Strategy. The sales team are doing little more than cold calling. This can be highly inefficient. A good Marketing Strategy opens the door for your sales team and provides them Marketing Collateral, such as brochures which include your Unique Selling Points, to help them close the sale. Sending your sales team out without a marketing strategy and support is like sending an army into battle without any weapons.

Once your marketing strategy generates the right sort of enquiries for your sales team, the selling begins. The receipt of enquiries is the start of your Sales Pipeline.

Does your Sales Pipeline leak? Every business' Sales Pipeline leaks to some extent. The correct question is: Have you done everything you can to ensure that it does not leak excessively? Do you even know what your Sales Pipeline looks like?

Very simply, a Sales Pipeline starts with an initial enquiry and ends with a sale. While the Sales Pipeline looks different in each business, there are still some similarities between them. In all businesses, there is a need to generate enquiries. This can be done through advertising, cold calling, public relations or word of mouth. This enquiry may be a phone call in response to an ad. Or, in retail, a customer may walk in your front door attracted by your shopfront marketing. This is the first step of the Sales Pipeline for any business. There are usually a number of steps from receiving an enquiry to generating a sale.

The next step might be getting an appointment with the prospective client to establish their needs. In a retail situation, the sales staff might ask: "Can I help you?" Once need is established, a second appointment may be made to present a proposal, or a quote may be provided. The final step in this generic Sales Pipeline would be to close the sale.

It is essential that every business owner understands their Sales Pipeline and where it leaks. Using the generic pipeline below (Figure 7.2), 50% of enquirers agree to an initial consultation. Then 80% of those agree to receive a formal proposal or ask for a quote. And finally, 50% of those who receive a formal proposal or quote, are converted to sales.

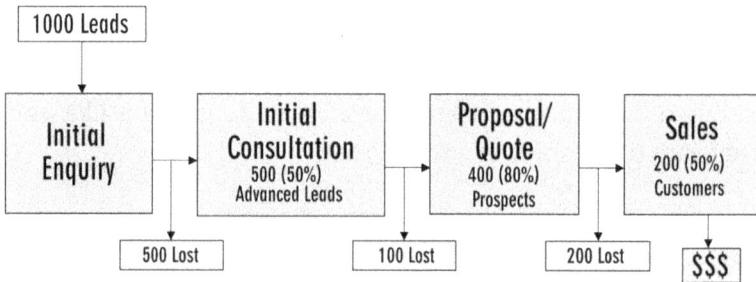

Figure 7.2 Sales Pipeline Example

By understanding each step in your Sales Pipeline, you can measure the success in moving prospects along the pipeline, and spot where your sales process needs to be improved.

No Sales Pipeline is leak proof. There are some people who you don't wish to become your customers. They may be the bargain hunters, the time wasters or people who are poor credit risks. So there should be a screening process to remove people who are not qualified to become your customers. To be effective, this screening process should remove unqualified prospects early in the pipeline, before you have invested too much time with them. But if you are turning away a high number of unqualified prospects, you should be looking at your enquiry generation strategy. If you sell luxury cruises, advertising in a tabloid newspaper will probably produce mostly unqualified enquiries.

All other prospects are, by definition, qualified, and their loss is one that you wish to minimise. If there is a large loss in getting that initial appointment, perhaps a script needs to be developed for staff to turn that initial enquiry into an appointment. If the losses are large in getting a request for a proposal or quotation, sales training on establishing rapport and need, creating desire and building value should be considered. If proposals (or quotations) have a low rate of acceptance, there could be a problem with the offer, or the way the sales person tried to close.

Put in place monitoring systems to measure the movements of prospects through your Sales Pipeline. Analyse the losses at each stage. By understanding your Sales Pipeline, you will understand what you are doing well, and where your pipeline leaks. Only then can you start plugging those leaks!

Action Steps

7.11 Define your Sales Pipeline

7.12 Start collecting data on your sales performance and analyse your Sales Pipeline results. What areas can you improve?

Your Average Value per Sale

Part of your offer to your customer will be in the way you package your services to increase the average value per sale. The most common strategies are the Upsell and Cross Sell. That is: "Do you want to Super Size that?", or "Do you want fries with that?" Other examples are: three for the price of two, a higher specification model, or a complete meal rather than a single course.

The best time to make another sale is when someone has already agreed to buy. One in three people when asked "Do you want fries with that?" say yes. The cost of supplying the fries— just some potatoes, is small compared with the price. The overheads are already covered through the initial purchase. And when you package products or services, you can afford to reduce your margins on the additional services, as you will still be increasing profit on the sale as long as you make some margin from the additional sale. This would be profit lost if the sale was not made at the time of the original purchase.

Successful businesses have already planned how they will package their products and services and will actively seek opportunities to increase the average sale value.

Action Steps

7.13 How could you package your services to increase the Average Value per Sale?

Increasing the times a Customer Buys

It is six times easier to sell to an existing customer than to a new customer. Having made a sale to a customer, you have a relationship and have increased their trust in your ability to satisfy their needs. All businesses should seek ways to increase the number of times a customer buys from them. This is the lowest cost marketing there is!

To make a customer return, it is firstly essential to make sure that they were fully satisfied with your initial sale. To do this you must have a customer satisfaction plan to ensure that your service is delivered at the level you expect every time. Then you need to make sure you stay in touch with them and give them a reason to come back. That is why newsletters are so popular, so you remain Top of Mind for the customer, so they think of you, when they are ready to buy again.

Understand the lifetime value of your customers. That is how much and how often they will buy from you over the length of time of their relationship with you. This may be 10 to 100 times the value of the initial sale, depending on the service.

For example, someone may stop by your coffee shop for a $4 café latte every day. This customer is potentially worth a $1000 per year to your business. Do you treat him as a $4 customer or a $1000 customer?

What are you doing to get that repeat service? Do you have a loyalty program? Do you have a 'Frequent Buyers Club' providing special offers to those that have been with you for a long time? What are you doing to recognise the value of your loyal customers and to show your appreciation to them?

Successful businesses do not assume that customers will continually return. They look for ways to make them feel special. They do extra things for them that others may not do. So if they do try someone else, they pretty quickly come back because the miss the extra service you provide.

Action Steps

How are you going to keep your customers coming back?

7.14 Define your customer service standards and policies.

7.15 Create a follow-up strategy with your customers.

Increasing Your Margins

Very simply, your margin is the price you sell at less the cost of the goods. This will include both materials and labour directly applied to the delivery of your products and services. You can increase your margins by increasing your prices or reducing your costs.

Most people understand how to reduce their costs, by being more efficient and by reducing the cost of their supplies; but what about increasing their prices?

When marketing a product or service, businesses find it difficult to set their prices. Too high, and no-one will buy, too low, everyone will buy, but you will go broke. So how do you set your prices?

The basic principle of pricing is that you should set your prices as high as the market will allow. (You may not decide to do this for other marketing reasons such as trying to buy customers, or offering an introductory price to encourage people to try a new product or service, but this should be a conscious strategic decision.)

When setting their prices, the single biggest mistake that businesses make is not to understand the value they offer compared with their competitors. So you must understand why your product is better than everyone else's.

Is it stronger? Does it last longer? Is it better designed? Does it look better? If it is a service, what are the superior results you provide? What is the value of such differences to the buyer?

If it is a commodity, then what else are you offering? For example, you can get a $2 fruit snack bar at the service station as you are filling your car. You know you could probably get the exact same bar for 25% less at the supermarket, but you will have to make a special stop, and then you will have to wait in a queue. It's just not worth the 50 cents you will save. You are prepared to pay 50 cents for the convenience of buying the bar now, when you are hungry! What if the bar was $5, would you buy it? Well you might if you knew that this service station was the only retail store for 200 kilometers!

Economists call this decision making "the cost of shoe leather" which is the amount of effort you are prepared to make (how far you will walk) to find a saving on your purchase.

When you understand the value of what you provide compared with your competitors, and that includes substitutes for your product or service, you can then better set your prices.

So if your product lasts twice as long, could you charge twice as much? Well consider the inconvenience factor of the replacement. If the item was socks, the inconvenience factor might be quite low. But if it was a special valve inside a jet engine, the replacement cost of which was many times the value of the valve, you could probably charge considerably more for the valve than twice the cost of a valve that lasts half as long, particularly if you guaranteed its lifetime.

So the value of the product has little to do with the cost of production or service. It is the value of the product to the buyer. However, it is not enough for you to know the value of the product or service to the buyer. The buyer has to know it as well — but it is surprising how often a buyer really doesn't understand the full value of what they may be buying.

If the buyer does not understand the value of what they are buying, they won't pay what it is worth. If they don't know there is not another retail store for 200 kilometers, they are unlikely to pay $5 for that snack bar. And the jet engine manufacturer may not understand the maintenance cost implications of a lower quality valve to the end user.

When you know what your product is truly worth, and you have educated the buyer on its value, you will be able to set prices that reflect that value. Ideally this is the maximum value that the buyer will bear — before they will decide they are better off with the lower value product, or the pain.

How do you find this threshold? Trial and error! Start at a price a little above the inferior product, but below a superior one, and keep lifting your prices until your conversion factor declines to an unsatisfactory level. If you can't sell it at a price above an inferior product, look closely at your marketing and sales process.

When businesses lift their prices, they are concerned that they will lose business. This is not necessarily a bad thing. Consider a business selling a service for $100 which they sell to 50 people a day. Let's say that the margin is $30. The profit would be $1500 per day. If they increase their prices by $10, what would happen if they lost 10% of their customers? Their profit would still have increased by $300 to $1800. They would actually need to lose more than 25% of their customers to be worse off.

If you can have a price rise that means you are making more money with less effort, isn't that a good thing? It will also give you more time to work on your business. If you are able to increase your prices and at the same time show increased value, you may even get more customers!

To understand this more fully, please use the Price — Profit Calculator from the Resources area.

Remember, if you don't understand your value, you will forever be just another commodity seller competing on price.

Action Steps

7.16 How can you save costs? Can you change suppliers? Negotiate bulk discounts? How can you become more efficient?

7.17 Examine your prices. Is there hidden value in your services that you can use to lift your prices?

The last point in your Marketing Plan, is to measure everything, and Test, Test, Test!

When you focus on the Five Profit Drivers, you will massively increase your business profitability. You will also be able to control the flow of activity in your business by managing your Sales Pipeline. Once you have a predictable flow of sales it is possible to streamline your operating systems.

Chris Wilson had a good look at his existing customer base. Basically he had taken on anyone that approached him, from small renovation jobs, to new houses and commercial work. He decided the most difficult clients were those with the smallest jobs. He also had problems charging them what he believed it was necessary to cover the time involved.

Chris had won awards for his small office blocks. These were being built in suburban centres as business was becoming more decentralised, and to meet the growing demand from new businesses. They became the offices of the new boutique firms that were appearing everywhere. They wanted to be located in modern stylish buildings, not too far from where their owners lived. His office, was in one of the buildings he designed. These clients also were very comfortable with his fees and understood the value he created for their business — offices that would attract premium rents in these suburban centres.

While Chris also enjoyed domestic design, he decided that the way forward was to only accept domestic jobs over a certain size, with clients who would appreciate what he provided (and would have no issue with his fees). However, his niche was to be the suburban business centres. He also found that often the owners of these buildings would want him to design their own homes, and would refer him to others of similar financial capacity. A good synergy.

When looking at his competitors, he noted that there were the big firms, like the one he walked out on! They tended to focus on the largest jobs, but did take on smaller ones that would be in Chris' marketplace, but they really did not show the flair that he did. Their top architects only worked on the largest projects.

Then there were the small architect businesses like his or smaller. They had all the problems his firm currently had in keeping up with the amount of business that came their way while providing a quality service to their clients. Then there were a few who were his true competitors in design ability, but their business skills were like his, before he took on his coach. They were cottage industries.

Chris' vision for his business was that he was going to offer a far more personal service than the big firms, but with more professional systems to ensure consistent quality that his smaller competitors lacked. He also felt that by presenting himself as a business centre design specialist, that this would win him more jobs in the niche he had selected.

The next step was to look at each of the profit drivers in his business. Firstly he analysed his enquiry sources. This was mostly through word-of-mouth, although he did a bit of advertising in magazines and of course he had a website. Unfortunately, the enquires from those sources were a trickle and of low quality.

His best buyers were the commercial developers. They did not look for architects online or in the magazines in which he advertised. He noted that those that came to him were through referrals. Chris knew he had to be much more active in his word-of-mouth marketing. This meant forming alliances and networking more than he had in the past, but in a very systematic way. He also knew his awards helped as well and he was not fully taking advantage of them. With his coach, Chris put together a detailed lead generation strategy for his business putting him right in front of his best buyers.

These strategies did increase his enquires, and now Chris knew he had to work on his sales process. His coach took his existing sales process, such as it was, and broke it into many more steps, with each step defined in detail. The coach also gave Chris training in how to close the sale. Chris discovered in this process that the sale is won far earlier in the process than he ever imagined. In some cases, even before he met the buyer.

Chris learnt how to demonstrate the value of his services to buyers in a way that meant price never was an issue. He also learnt how to increase the value of the sale by adding extra services and providing packages. He found out how to increase repeat business with various follow-up strategies. Finally, he understood how to increase his prices without losing income.

Altogether, Chris now had a marketing plan. He was getting more of the right kind of clients, he could increase his prices, and he could see where his next business was coming from. For the first time he felt in charge of his marketing and was now confident about hiring new staff.

Actions Steps

7.18 Put together your strategies from this chapter for each of the Profit Drivers. Use the targets from the Profit Driver Calculator (see Resources section) to identify the gap between your existing performance for each Profit Driver and your goal. Beside each Target write out your strategy for achieving it.

Use the table at the end of the chapter to summarise your Marketing Plan.

One Page Marketing Plan

Profit Driver	Today	Action Plan to Achieve Goal	One Year Later
No. Enquires			
Conversion to Sales			
Average Value / Sale			
No. Repeat Purchases			
Gross Profit / Sale			

Strategy Summary

Unique Selling points	
Best Buyers	
Strategy 1	
Strategy 2	
Strategy 3	
Strategy 4	

Chapter 8

Pillar Three – Business Systems

Many studies have shown that businesses with weak systems seldom achieve efficiencies above 66%. While 100% efficiency is impossible to achieve, a good system can easily increase efficiency by up to 30%. The financial cost of not having a good business system is obvious. What is not so obvious is the impact of poor systems on your customers. The total profit lost can easily be double this amount when you account for the loss of sales.

Without a good Business System, the business owner does not own a Business, just a job with overheads! Without a Business System, you will never have a business that runs without you.

Do You Own a Business or a Job?

Answer the following questions honestly:

- How many hours do you work a week?
- When was the last time you took an uninterrupted holiday?
- Do your staff have a better job than you?

Now ask yourself:

Do I Own a Business or a Job — with Overheads?

Are you happy about the answers to these questions?

In my experience, too many owners, after investing their time and money, have not got a fair return from their business. They are making ends meet (well some are), but are they getting what they deserve for the effort they make? Think about it this way. Take the money you have put into your business, and take the time you have put in as well. If you had invested those funds wisely, and got a nine-to-five job, would you be better or worse off? Consider also the headaches of running your own business?

So what should be a reasonable return on your business? After you pay yourself a wage, you should be returning a 25-30% of your asset investment value. The benchmark is the return purchasers of a good franchise should expect. A more risky business should have an even higher return — or else you can play it safe with a franchise. This means that if you were to sell your business today, you should get at least 3 times its annual profit. Too often, the business owner is their business, and if he or she were to leave it for even a short time, there would be a sharp decline in its profits. No-one will pay them for what is a personal business.

There are two lessons that must be learned before you can have a business that won't stay small and is of value to someone else. You must Value Your Time, and Manage by Reports.

Valuing Your Time

In this section we will address the single biggest reason why small businesses stay small. Many people who are Micro-Stayers, especially professionals, find this a difficult topic to apply. It is a problem that is rampant throughout small business.

What I will look at first is the typical mindset of a small business owner and how it stops them from growing. Next I will discuss some alternative approaches to this mindset, including strategies for solopreneurs and those in professional practice, and finally I will present some practical strategies to address these issues.

In the earlier chapters I talked about the fundamentals of business success. But we all know what we should be doing:

- Setting goals
- Creating plans
- Measuring results etc

We know what we should do but don't do it— why?

We are too busy doing routine tasks, including fire-fighting. Routine is known and comfortable. We can feel very busy just doing the routine tasks, even have a feeling that we have achieved something by the end of the day, but at the end of the week, at the end of the month, at the end of the year, nothing has changed.

We know we should be working on the business instead of in it, but how can we when we have all routine tasks to complete? If we don't do them, who will? And you ask yourself — "How can I get anyone to do it the way I want it done, and how can I afford to pay them? I am just making ends meet and I am working 60 hours a week already."

Does any of this sound familiar?

So we have some fantastic excuses ready to go, on why we shouldn't spend time on the riskier, more challenging strategic tasks. When we stick to the routine, we know if we do certain things, we get certain results. The results don't change, and it doesn't get any easier, but it's comfortable.

This is how most small business owners think. It creates a trap from which they cannot escape unless they think in a different way. When you work on your business, you have to let go of some of the routine tasks, and spend time working on your strategies. In the short term you might even lose sales, as well as see your expenses increase.

Looking at where you are today, you might ask how can you escape this trap? Have a look at other businesses in your industry. Do you see businesses there that are 2x, 3x, 10x your size? How do you think they got there? Doing what you are doing today? The owners of these businesses have many more things to worry about than you do, but they still manage.

Every one of them only has the same 24 hours a day you have, the same 7 days a week. They each just have two hands. So what is the difference between these business owners and you? How have they grown their business, while you struggle?

The answer is in how they choose to spend their time. What they decide to do. And what they decide to have others to do for them. Let me give you an example:

Let's look at what a Brain Surgeon does:

Most business owners I talk to believe almost everything they do in their business, only they can do. They have learnt from experience if they give work to someone else, it gets messed up, and then they spend twice as long fixing things.

This is not what Brain Surgeons do. When they operate on a patient, they are not in charge of the operating theatre — this is the responsibility of the theatre nurse. Brain surgeons don't open up the patient, or close. They leave that to a junior surgeon. Everything is prepared for them, and someone else mops up the blood from the floor later. All they do is the brain surgery, and some marketing before hand (client needs), and marketing afterwards (client satisfaction).

How is this possible?

Hospitals have very sophisticated systems, and everyone is highly trained in their use. There are checks and counter-checks. Nothing is left to chance. The very expensive surgeon, the most highly trained person in the theatre, only does what he or she has been trained to do. They don't waste their time doing jobs others can do. In other words they don't spend dollar time on penny jobs. The brain surgeon only does the brain surgery, and a bit of marketing.

This is, of course, a rather simplistic description of a brain surgeon's job. The point of this is for business owners to understand where the real brain surgery is in their business. The part of their job that is most valuable to their business, which for most business owners, is only a very small part of their time.

Examples of brain surgery are: the marketing of your business, the relationships with your key customers, or if you are a consultant, the analysis of the problem you have been asked to solve. Not data entry, or possibly even data collection, and not the bookkeeping. The challenge for business owners is to identify what part of their role is brain surgery. Theoretically, everything else can and should be delegated or outsourced. This way you can spend more time on what generates your business income.

A great theory, but how can you make this happen in the real world?

Business Systems. When you delegate or outsource to someone, you need to document what the person will receive and what they will return to you, complete with standards and the form in which they will provide it to you. Then all involved need training in the system. This takes some work, but for a small investment in your time, the dividends are huge.

The theatre nurse does not know how to do brain surgery, but they know before the operation, what equipment the surgeon will need, and when they will need it. They will also know how to prepare the theatre and the patient. Detailed procedures will have been developed so everyone in the theatre will know their role, and the brain surgeon will have optimised his or her time doing what they have been specifically trained to do.

When you know where the brain surgery is in your business, you will be able to leverage your time. You will spend more time with your customers, and more time working on your business, rather than in it. Ultimately, you will have a business that runs without you.

How many times have you heard a fellow business owner say that they are the chief cook & bottle washer— and wear that as a badge of pride. May be that's what you do as well.

I had a builder client who spent up to an hour a day ferrying plans around town. I asked him why he didn't use a courier. His answer was: "Couriers cost money." I had a colleague who would regularly go to pick up mail at his post office box, rather than have it sent to his home address. That would take him potentially an hour or two a week. He was trying to save on the redirection cost.

In each case, the business owner placed no value on their time. If they really thought that their time was of equal value as the time of a courier, why not get a job as a courier? They would also be able to sleep a lot easier at night. Neither of these people considered that alternative as a realistic option, as they believed they could make much more in their business than being a courier. Yet they did take on the job as a courier in their own business. They had not put a value on their time.

So what other jobs are you doing in your business that can be done by someone else?

Do you do your own books? Most small business owners do. They spend hours on something they hate and at which they are not very good. They make mistakes, which they then pay an accountant to fix. While they do this, they are not talking to their customers, or out there finding new ones, but they think they are saving themselves money. Even if you are good at the books, do you want to be known as the owner with a great set of books, or as the owner who spends more time with their customers?

There is no point doing well what you shouldn't be doing at all.

Think about it this way. If you brought in a bookkeeper, you are bringing in someone who knows how to prepare your accounts for your high priced accountant. They will probably pay for themselves by the amount they save in accountants' fees. They will probably do it in half the time you will because that is their brain surgery.

While they are doing the books, can you be servicing a client? A bookkeeper charges $30-40/hour. How much can you make in that hour? Maybe you have a bookkeeper already. Great, but what else are you doing that you shouldn't?

Here are two ways you can value your time. The first is a way that all business owners should feel most comfortable. If you were not doing your own books, if you were not taking out your own garbage, what would you be doing? Providing a service to a greater number of clients? Making more sales? How much money could you be making if you weren't taking out the garbage? Say you could earn $100 per hour, but you still did your own books. You are not saving yourself $30-40 an hour. You are costing yourself $60-70 per hour, and if your bookkeeper can do it twice as fast as you can, it is costing you a lot more.

Don't think about how much you are saving when you take out your own garbage, think how much it is costing you!

Now the second way to value your time — this method is for entrepreneurs. Don't you believe that if you had just an extra 2 hours a week to actually work on your business for one year, rather than in it, that your business would be transformed? How much is that time worth? Let's say you had a goal to add $100,000 to the bottom line of your business in the next 12 months, which you would achieve by spending 2 hours a week working on your business by educating yourself, creating strategies, planning, and implementing systems. Two hours a week, for a year — to earn an extra $100,000. Don't you believe you would achieve that goal if you used that time in that way?

If you did, your time would be worth $1000 per hour! That's how an entrepreneur would value their time. Can you afford someone now to do your books and take out your garbage? Can you afford someone to show you how to do all this?

Place a Value on Your Time or you will forever be busy, taking out your own garbage.

Action Steps

8.1 Place a value on your time. If you had an extra hour each day, how much money could you make in that hour? How many more sales might you be able to make? Could you use that time to work on your business to achieve your goals?

8.2 Keep a diary and work out where you are spending your time. Is it all brain surgery— I bet it isn't. Keep a Yuk list. The tasks you hate doing — this is the easiest work to give away. If you can get someone to do the job at less than your time is worth, and you still do the job — it is costing you money!

Managing by Reports

As a business grows, the more moving parts it has. When you are trying to juggle ever more balls in the air it becomes more difficult to keep an eye on everything that's happening. Then the balls start to drop. Does your business have as many moving parts as a Jumbo Jet? How do jet pilots manage?

When a business starts-up, because of the risk of failure, the owner has to watch everything. Fortunately, when you start-up, there is not a lot to watch! But it is hard to get out of the habit, which is why so many business owners continue to micromanage the business as it gets larger. Now if you could keep your eye on every ball in the air that might be ok. But at some point it becomes impossible to maintain, with owners focussing on where they feel most comfortable, rather than on what is most important.

Studies have shown that there are limits to how many different things a human being can monitor and react to. This of course, varies from person to person, but everyone has their limit. For example, only the most highly skilled jugglers can keep more than six balls in the air. So when we try to keep our eye on everything, we will start dropping balls.

So how does a jet pilot keep an eye on everything? Funnily enough, they have six gauges in the cockpit, representing the key areas of the plane's performance. Or in business speak, the plane's Key Performance Indicators. These are the most vital factors in keeping the plane in the air. So if the seat 57D does not fully recline, or the airline logo paint is starting to flake on the body of the plane, they do not know about it. They have the flight attendants and the maintenance engineers to worry about such problems. These personnel are highly trained to notify the pilots if there is something they should worry about. The pilot trusts these personnel to do their job and follow their procedures, and only advise on matters that affect the plane's safety. All the pilots need to do is concentrate on flying the plane.

What if there is an engine problem? The plane's flight management system is set up so that any problem with a key part in the flight system will be evident on the high level gauges. If there is a drop in airspeed, the pilot will query the system to determine which of the many causes may be responsible. They are able to drill down from the high level gauge which has moved from the safe area to investigate which of the plane's subsystems may be a fault. In almost all cases, the pilot is able to identify and either correct the problem or take action that will enable the plane to land safety. If pilots worried about every little non-critical problem on the plane, the chances are they might only notice the big ones when it was too late to do anything about them.

In business, the owner might identify that their cash reserves are declining. (Cash at Hand is one of the biggest Key Performance Indicators for any business.) Having seen this, the owner might ask the accountant to look at their detailed reports to identify the cause. Is it due to slow sales, overdue payments by debtors, cost blow-outs or overinvestment in inventory?

Having identified cost blowouts as the cause, the accountant might ask the operations manager why costs have gone up. She might advise that a maintenance problem has caused the over-run. When the operations manager speaks to the maintenance superintendent, she may discover the problem was caused by poor quality feedstock. In other words, a cash problem was caused by supplier quality control problem. Further analysis is of course, possible. The owner has therefore uncovered a critical supplier problem by interrogating staff after a key performance indicator has moved from the safe zone.

By having a small number of Key Performance Indicators which define the health of a business, and which are linked to other more detailed reports, the owner can fly their business using just a few gauges. If there is a deeper problem in the business it will become visible. As an owner with an excellent Business Management System is confident that they will identify problems in a timely fashion, they can focus on flying their business towards their ultimate objective which is their real job.

When you have reports created by a Business Management System, you don't have to be there every day.

Some typical Key Performance Indicators (KPI's) that are critical for most businesses are:

Common Financial KPI's are:

- Cash at hand
- Creditors
- Debtors
- Profit
- Inventory

Common Marketing KPI's are:

- Sales
- Cost per Sale
- Number of Enquiries
- Cost per Lead
- Conversion Rate
- Upsales / Crosssales / Backend sales
- Repeat Business

Common Operational KPI's are:

- Units produced
- Unit Costs
- Returns / Customer Complaints
- Uptime
- Stock-outs
- Production targets

Common Human Resource KPI's are:

- Staff Turnover
- Training Goals met
- Staff satisfaction survey results
- Staff appraisals completion rate

Common Safety & Environment KPI's are:

- Lost Time Injuries
- Medical Treatments
- Near Misses
- Regulatory Compliance Performance
- Environmental Emissions
- Spills
- Recycle Targets

By creating reports for each of the key areas of your business, you are able to manage your business without being there every day, and your business will run without you.

Action Steps

8.3 Identify the Key Performance Indicators for your business.

8.4 Determine how your Management Reports will be produced, how often and by whom.

Creating a Business System

By building a Business System you are able to maximise the value of your time, and create reports that will make your business independent of you. Even if you are a one-man-band, there is still a lot you can do to separate yourself from your business, by creating passive income streams, and leveraging your knowledge.

Business owners who own a job, already know they do. (Don't you!) They know they spend all their time working in their business, not on their business, and their reason for not doing anything about this, is that they say they are too busy. However, if they saw an opportunity to double their income, they would find the time! So it is actually about whether the rewards that come from their business running on auto-pilot are sufficiently attractive to them to find the time. If they still can't find the time they should never again complain about their business running their lives, as it is clearly not that important!

A good system is logical and simple to use, and ensures that your customer service levels are always consistent. Some of the other key benefits of a business system, are:

- Systems enable your business to operate without you
- Systems turn your business into a money making machine
- Systems increase business effectiveness and efficiency
- Systems allow you to develop a saleable asset
- Systems take out most of the risk of a business, by operating it with proven methods of carrying out its activities
- Systems allow you to employ staff with lower levels of skills
- Systems simplify training of staff and speed up the time for them to become productive, profitable employees
- Systems enable you to leverage your time, your effort, your knowledge and your money

A good system guides companies to manage and monitor their activity. It will produce a consistent and predictable return for the money, time and effort invested by an owner. This system will give you control of your business even if you are not there. Your system will be based around policies, planning and procedures in every part of your business that you and your staff will apply every day.

A Business System does not have to be complex — good ones aren't! However, they are also essential if you want to grow your business. Many businesses fail as they expand or change their focus, because their systems are inadequate, and quality declines as they try to service more customers.

The first step to build a business system is to look at the key areas of your business. Typical Key Business Areas are listed below:

- Strategic Business Development
- Management
- People
- Financial
- Marketing
- Administration
- Legal
- Information Technology
- Operations
- Risk Management

Below these high level key business areas will be a number of sub-areas, such as Lead Generation and Follow-up Strategies under Marketing.

The next step is to undertake a Workflow Process Analysis from the time a customer phones your business, until you bank their cheque (Figure 8.1). Break the steps down to the point that the 'non-brain surgery' parts can be identified and can be delegated to others. Align this to your key business areas. This will allow you to understand where you add most value to your business.

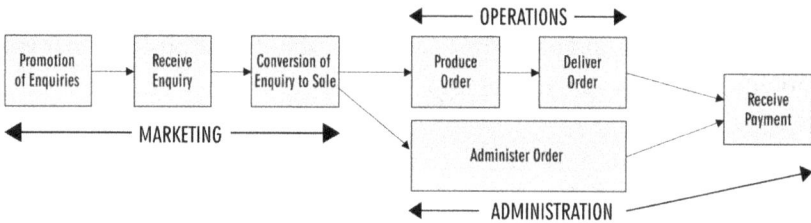

Figure 8.1 Example of a Workflow Process Analysis

Each of the tasks needs to be documented using systems tools such as:

- Procedures
- Templates
- Checklists
- Scripts

These should be included into the appropriate key business area.

Roles then should be allocated to the key business areas and activities in the Workflow Process, and finally people assigned to the roles.

A good business system will enable you to:

- produce an operational manual for your business,
- produce staff (and contractor) position descriptions,
- act as a training tool for new staff, and
- provide performance measurement.

The way you make your business run without you is to create a business management system that allows you to run it by reports. The reports are specified within the business system, along with how and when they are produced. When you set up such a system, you no longer need to be involved in every part of your business.

Once your system is implemented, your work will decrease and your results will increase. You will also have created a valuable asset that can operate without you.

When you have a Business System, you have an Exit Strategy!

Often staff can feel threatened by this. They might ask: "How will this affect my job? Might I be replaced?" The answer to such questions is to show them what's in it for them. This is covered in the next section—People Systems.

Chris now had to think about better use of his time. He did have an assistant, and a draftsman, but he knew he was not time efficient. He was micromanaging his staff because he was never really sure they understood what he wanted. Chris also suspected he was still doing work that he shouldn't. His coach asked him to keep a time log. When he looked at it he was shocked at how little time he spent on the "Brain Surgery" of his business.

His coach then asked him to value his time, based on what he wanted to earn, and the time he wanted to work. When Chris did the calculation, he not only realised he was undercharging, but that he could easily afford to bring in more staff, as long as he used the time he freed up, to work ON his business.

He was able to use his time log to create descriptions of roles for others he could bring into his business. He also looked in more detail at his design process. Chris was able to identify several key points where his input was critical for the creative result he wanted. He discovered that a large part of what he was doing could be done by a junior architect, as long as he had very clear procedures to follow.

Gradually Chris added more professional staff to his business, and even added a supervisor. This was a little scary at first, but once he mapped out the workflow process, he was able to properly define the role. He put in checks and reporting so that he could monitor the results without having to peer over people's shoulders all the time. He also had procedures for just about everything, so the staff knew how he wanted things, and there was a consistency in the service they provided whether he was there or not. He had regular staff meetings which were structured to provide the reports he need to feel comfortable the work was being done to his satisfaction.

At this stage, his coach insisted that the two of them would hold regular "board meetings" — his coach was taking a non-executive director role, holding him accountable. His coach insisted that Chris provide him with reports beforehand, and at the meetings asked him a lot of *tough questions about his business. Their meetings became far more strategically focused. The coach was no longer too interested in the daily operations of his business, as long as Chris met his targets!*

Chris now knew what working on his business really meant. He now felt he was in control of it. So Chris and Kate took an overseas holiday with the boys, and he knew that when he returned, his business would have carried on as if he had not left.

Action Steps

8.5 Identify the Key Business Areas and sub-areas for your business.

8.6 Analyse your Workflow Process and assign the steps to the Key Business Areas.

8.7 Create Procedures, Templates, Checklists and Scripts for each part of your business that describe in detail how the activities in the Workflow Process are undertaken.

8.8 Assign roles to the Key Business Areas and activities in the Workflow Process.

8.9 Assign people to the roles. Note in a small business it is quite usual that a person undertakes more than one role!

Chapter 9

Pillar Four – People Systems

People are the number one reason for long-term business success or failure. So this is the most important part of your Business System. Business owners are often concerned about how their staff will react when they implement a system, and there are plenty of examples where it hasn't worked. However, the primary reasons for this failure are that staff have not been involved in the development of the systems, they feel that their jobs might be threatened, and no-one has explained what's in it for them!

Staff benefits from the implementation of systems include:

- Additional training and skill development
- Increased pay from higher productivity
- Increased security as their company becomes financially stronger
- Greater opportunities in a dynamic organisation
- Improved and less stressful work environment
- A happier boss!

Even if you don't have staff, similar processes are required for contractors, and even suppliers.

I still hear some bosses say: "If I train my staff they will leave and I will have wasted my time and money". Well, what if you don't train them and they stay! The truth is good people are actually more likely to stay when you have great People Systems.

I also hear: "You just can't get good people these days". Nowadays potential employees are just as fussy about whom they work for, as employers are about whom they hire, and if you don't have good people systems, the best people won't join your firm, or won't stay. This is not just about money. People will actually work for less pay if there are good people systems in a business and the owner has a clear vision for their business.

There is a large cost incurred by a business for a wrong hire or when someone quits. When you properly account for lost time, money, disruption to operations, impact on customer satisfaction and effort to replace them, this cost is up to one and a half times the departing employee's wage. With current high employment levels and an estimated 25% of the workforce saying in surveys they are thinking of changing jobs over the next twelve months, it's not hard to see why hiring the right staff and keeping them has become a major focus for many business owners.

It is important to understand why people leave their jobs. Pay is not the number one reason. Most people quit their boss, not their jobs! A recent survey showed that the top reasons people left their jobs were:

1. Overall dissatisfaction with the job
2. Dissatisfaction with the type of work
3. Lack of opportunities for advancement
4. Dissatisfaction with the boss
5. Dissatisfaction with pay

All the top reasons are due to bad management. These reasons can be addressed with good people management systems.

Key features of good people systems are they:

- Define your Organisation now and in the future
- Define the roles in your organisation
- Identify the required skills for each role
- Determine Performance Benchmarks
- Review Performance
- Have training programs for your people
- Have Performance Reward Programs

By formalising your organisation, and the roles of each of your employees, there is much better understanding and accountability of the tasks for which they are responsible. It is also much easier to define training needs for each employee.

A typical organisation for any business has three main functions (Figure 9.1). The Managing Director or CEO reports to the board which set strategic policy and profit objectives. The CEO runs the company by reports (3rd Pillar). Within the organisation, any organisation, there are three parts

- Marketing (finds the customers and makes the sales)
- Administration (manages the sale)
- Operations (delivers the sale)

Note this very sales focused construction of the business, because whatever your business, you are in the Selling Business.

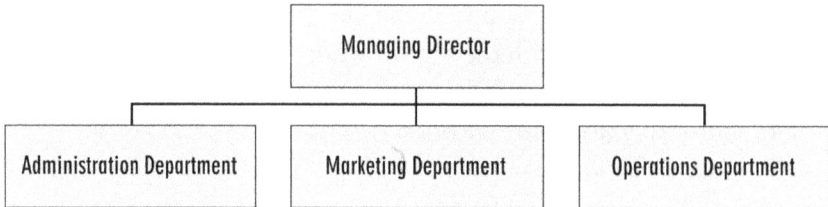

Figure 9.1 The fundamental parts of a business

Now a small business doesn't have 'departments'. There may be only few people in the business. Maybe only one! But this organisation structure is about the roles in your business which are to be aligned with your Workflow Process. In any business, no matter how small it is, these roles exist. Starting to recognise all these roles, even if it is you doing them all, is an important first step in organising your business. Below each of the departments there will be a number of sub-roles such as — Accounts Receivable, Accounts Payable and Accountant roles under Administration.

List the tasks in each of the key areas. Create performance benchmarks for each task. For example, invoices must be issued within two business days. There should be 10 sales calls per week.

When benchmarks are established, there is also a better understanding of the difference between good and poor performance, and an objective basis with which to measure it. It is also possible to reward good performance and put in place development plans where the performance does not reach the benchmark.

The next step is assigning people to roles. Typically in small business people are performing more than one role, but as your business grows, these roles will be filled by individuals. Some of the roles may be performed by contractors or other people outside your organisation, but you must recognise how the work is being done in your business.

People Systems will also contain a range of other policies, such as staff induction, overtime, annual leave etc. In this way, your staff has a clear understanding of their entitlements, and you will avoid the pitfalls of inconsistent application of your policies — often a source of workplace tension. The most important reason to have People Systems is:

Good People Systems attract and keep Good People.

So if you ever want your business to run without you, you must have good people.

Chris was nervous at first at bringing in people with a similar level of experience as himself. They tended to challenge his way of doing things more often. The funny thing was, that often they were right! Before he hired his staff, Chris' coach insisted that he had described their roles and had an operations manual for their position when they started.

When he took this advice, he found that the amount of time he spent in showing people the ropes was greatly reduced. It also enabled his staff to cover more easily for each other's absences.

Chris also made sure he spent time with his staff to explain the targets for his business. He made sure they understood their own role in reaching those targets and reviewed their performance regularly with them. When they performed well, there were rewards, and when the did not perform as expected, he determined what help they needed in reaching the targets. Sometimes it was some additional training, and other times it meant that they needed to review they way things were working in the business.

His staff was now as enthusiastic about his business as he was. They could see how the business was succeeding, knew their part in its success, and shared in the rewards.

Action Steps

9.1 Use your Business System to produce Position Descriptions for each role.

9.2 Create a performance standard for each activity within the role. These should be based on your businesses goals. For example, a sales goal might determine a performance standard for the number of sales calls and the conversion rate for enquiries.

9.3 Create reports to monitor individual achievement of these goals.

9.4 Set-up a performance appraisal process with your staff to review progress to their goal achievement. This should include a review of their training needs and their career aspirations.

9.5 Have a process for recognition of good performance, and counselling for under performance.

9.6 Create an induction & training manual for new staff.

9.7 Develop a policy manual for all staff situations, eg overtime, sick leave, hours of work, dress code etc.

9.8 Have a staff communication strategy. For example, do you have formal weekly meetings?

Chapter 10

Pillar Five – You!

The previous Four Pillars of Business Success have been focused on business know-how. While this is vitally important, all the knowledge in the world is not going to assist you if you are not prepared to use it. It's like buying an exercise bike, and never using it. Possessing the bike, without using it, will not cause you to get fit or lose weight.

Knowledge on its own does not produce success either. For instance, the universities are full of academics with large amounts of business knowledge. There are professors who know how to analyse marketing strategy using the most sophisticated techniques in the most complex markets, and yet, they remain on an academics salary rather than use their knowledge to build their own business and make money. Now it is true that some remain in this role because their interest is the pursuit of knowledge, but they also are the first to say that academics should be paid more.... from the taxes raised from people who run and work in successful businesses.

Conversely, there are many entrepreneurs who have had little formal education, but have been very successful. Richard Branson was functionally illiterate due to dyslexia when he left school, but he had the drive, and the passion. He knew he did not need to know everything, as long as he was prepared to seek advice from others who knew more.

So it is not just about knowledge. It is about passion to achieve some goal. This passion is driven by a vision of the business that inspires the owner. People who don't achieve their goals in business have some other priority. Success always comes with some price tag. It may be investing money in a business, rather than an overseas trip. It might be the long hours, postponing personal pleasures until a goal is achieved. It might

103

mean taking a drop in income while learning new skills. It might mean moving beyond the comfort zone and taking some personal risks — the risk and embarrassment of failure.

Chris Wilson, in the decay phase in our story of a business earlier on, did not have the passion. He did not want to do the things he knew he had to do to achieve the results he wanted. In the end, he really didn't need the money, as Kate was bringing in the income, and there were definitely attractions in spending more time at home. So there was nothing to drive him out of his comfort zone to take the risks to make his business grow. Whether he realized it or not, Chris had chosen the course his business had taken, because he was not prepared to take another.

To achieve something you have never achieved before, you must do something you have never done before. You must become someone you have never been before. You will also have to pay a price measured in terms of sacrifice, time, effort and personal discipline.
Answer the following questions:

What is your Goal? Be as specific as possible. For example: "I want to increase my profit by $100,000 in the next 12 months." Don't worry about how you will achieve your goal yet, just write down your goal. If you are having difficulty with this, please use the Business Goals Generator Tool that is listed in the Resources area.

What benefit does this goal bring you? Types of benefits include:

- Money
- Time
- Recognition
- Personal fulfillment
- Support to others
- Well being to yourself and / or others

It is usually a mixture of these factors.

What is stopping you from achieving this goal? Some of the obstacles could be:

- Money
- Time
- Lack of knowledge
- Commitments to others
- Personal obstacles

Some obstacles, of course, are often a result of something deeper. For example, money may only be an obstacle because you don't know how to raise it, and similarly, 'having the time' may also be due to a lack of knowledge on how to manage it. Just about all obstacles, even personal ones, come down to lack of knowledge in how to address the problem.

What are you prepared to sacrifice to achieve your goal? Every goal has a price. The bigger the goal, the bigger the price. What is the price for your goals? For each sacrifice you will make, state the benefit. Some examples are:

- I will keep my current car for another two years and take a local holiday rather than an international one so we have sufficient funds to invest in the refurbishment of our store to attract new customers, and keep old ones!
- I won't go away this Christmas so we can create our new product range for next year which will allow us to lift our prices.
- I will give up the next 10 Saturdays to undertake a business course which will help me in my marketing, so I can increase our sales.
- I will pay for a business coach to show me how to organise my business so I can work shorter hours and take a holiday.

As most obstacles are knowledge based, they can be overcome with education and advice. So how much should you spend on education versus advice? It depends on how core the information is to the business, and how fast you want to go. For example, most businesses don't need to know how to design a website, and will pay for someone to build it for them rather than learning how to build one themselves. Marketing, however, is critical for any business, so education with a course or through coaching would be a better approach. That does not mean you won't hire a copywriter to create your ads, but you do need to deeply understand your Unique Selling Points and the ultimate benefits of your service to your Best Buyers before you hire one.

In Chris Wilson's case, his obstacle was leaving his comfort zone and changing the way he worked. How could he have overcome this? He could have created a vision for which he was passionate to increase his desire sufficiently, or else he could have sought coaching to help him create the vision and planning so he could move out from the comfort zone. Chris had already done some business courses, but it was not enough for him. A business coach would have been an appropriate course of action to try next, but in Chris' mind, this would be a cost, and anyway, it might not work.

> *"If you think You can, or think You can't —*
> *You will be right either way"* — Henry Ford

A very common example of a barrier that business owners face is fear of public speaking, which can be an obstacle that prevents them from utilising an important strategy to increase exposure for their business. The solution in that case would be to either join Toastmasters, an organisation dedicated to showing people how to talk in front of others, or hire a public speaking coach.

The choice on how you obtain your knowledge also depends on the value you place on your time. If that value is high, you will be prepared to pay a premium for quick access to expertise that will be specific to your business issues. If that value is low, maybe buying (or borrowing) a book is best for you. While this cost will be low (or zero), the information will be more general, with no direct support. As in everything, there is a trade-off in education between time and cost. If you access that knowledge sooner, what would be the value to you?

If you have trouble identifying what you might sacrifice to achieve your goal, this would be an indication that your goal is not of sufficient priority for you to make sacrifices for it. There is nothing wrong with this. Everyone has different priorities. So revisit your goal, and create one that you are prepared to make the sacrifices required.

Now some will say: "I would be happy to make the sacrifice if I was absolutely certain that it would work." These people are seeking the 'Silver Bullet'. The Secret to Business Success. For them I suggest the next chapter.

If you have created an objective for which you are passionate, you will be prepared to make the sacrifice, and make the commitment to see it through until you achieve your goal.

These are the steps:

1. You start with your goal.

2. This creates passion.

3. Passion overcomes obstacles because you will seek out answers through advice and education.

4. When knowledge and passion are combined, everything else gives way to your goal. You will be prepared to Pay the Price the goal demands.

That is the guarantee of business success.

Chris had set out his goals. He understood that his biggest obstacle to his goal was lack of business knowledge. He was prepared to invest in his own development and business education. Although he would have to pay for this, his goal was important enough to him that he was prepared to make the sacrifice to achieve it. He was also ready to listen to advice, and act on it when he understood how it would help.

Chris was able to overcome his biggest obstacle to success. Himself. He had learnt the lessons of the Five Pillars and he had applied them. For a time he felt distinctly uncomfortable, but with the advice and support of his coach, and his determination to achieve his goals, Chris persevered.

There were many things Chris had to change. Not everything worked, and some things took longer to implement than he expected, but his perseverance paid off, and month by month, the results came.

Chris was able to achieve his three year goals in less than two. He had a business that did not depend on him. It was achieving his profitability goal and growing at a rate at which he was comfortable.

This success had enabled Chris to develop an exit strategy for his business. It was now an asset in which others would want to invest. This had already started. He was offering his senior staff shares in his business as a reward for their performance, and when he was ready, he would allow them to buy him out. Chris was now making more than he had ever done before, while working less and having a lot more fun.

Chris thought back on what would have happened if he had not made those critical decisions when he abandoned his comfort zone. He still ran into those he considered his competitors all those years ago, and saw they were struggling. When asked, he was happy to share his knowledge, but they kept on doing the same things, still searching for the Secret of Business Success.

Action Steps

10.1 Write out your goal. Be as detailed as you can. Particularly if it is a large one. What are the steps?

10.2 Write out the obstacles to your goal.

10.3 Write out what you are prepared to sacrifice to achieve your goal.

Part Three

Getting Results

Chapter 11

The Secret of Business Success

As business owners, we are continually bombarded with unbelievable promises of get rich quick schemes. It seems, every day some one has discovered some amazing secret formula that they are willing to share with you, which will make you millions, for just $99.95...plus tax of course.

You know, if I had a secret formula on how to make millions, I wouldn't be selling it for $99.95. (Many of these schemes just show you how to sell to others what you just bought!)

Everyone is looking for a success formula— a 'Silver Bullet'. Maybe a recipe that you can follow, like the ones you see in books by TV chefs. Isn't it funny that when you follow the recipe, the result never looks quite like the picture in the book?

Why don't these recipe books work for most people? The problem is usually not with the recipe. It is that each step in the recipe is actually several steps which assume a certain level of skill. It's like giving someone who has never driven a car, a map on how to get from one side of the country to the other. There is nothing wrong with the directions, but they do assume you know how to drive a car.

So why are there so many of these offers? It is because people who are addicted to the Business Opportunity Three-step keep throwing money at them. What is the Business Opportunity Three-step?

1. Irrational exuberance at finding the secret formula to business success.

2. Disenchantment when they find that the formula requires hard work, persistence and a step out of their comfort zone, and results are not instantaneous.

3. Frustration and Blame for others when they find the formula does not work for them when they stop following the formula.

Those addicted to the Three-Step never stop looking for the secret formula, and never stick with any formula long enough for it to work.

But first, let us take a step backwards and ask — what is success?

You could define success as being recognised by others for your achievements.

Or

You could define it as achieving what you want to achieve.

I prefer the second definition. People generally regarded as successful have their own personal motivation. Whether their goal was a worthy cause, or business success, recognition by others was usually not the motivation, although that may occur as a by-product of their success.

Some people believe luck has a lot to do with success. Being in the right place at the right time. So let's take an example of extreme good luck — winning the lottery. No effort, just luck. Yet studies of lottery winners have shown most blow their good fortune in under two years, and not to mention the alienation of friends and relatives making for many, their life a misery.

When Samuel Goldwyn of MGM fame, was asked was luck a part of his success, he answered, "well there may have been some luck, but the funny thing was, the harder I worked, the luckier I got!"

So I think we can agree that luck has little to do with success.

So what are the keys to success?

They are the Five Pillars we have covered in this book, the final Pillar — You, being the most important. As only You can supply the passion, commitment and drive for success.

Talk to any successful person you know, or read their books, and it is the same formula. They started with a vision for their business about which they were passionate. They didn't wait for luck, they created a plan. This enabled them to understand the value of their time, and importance in gaining knowledge.

The next step was to have a Marketing Strategy for their business. They didn't just open their doors, and hope that someone would walk in and buy. They needed to have systems that would ensure their efficiency, effectiveness and profitability, and make their business independent of them. And they needed people management systems as all successful businesses depend on other people for their success. How often have you heard CEO's say that our people are our greatest asset?

When you hear all this, you may be saying to yourself: "This is nothing new. I know all this. What I am looking for is the secret formula. The short cut to success without all the hard work. Where is the 'Silver Bullet'?"

Well I will let you in to the secret shortly, but before I do, I would like to mention a book by Napoleon Hill called "Think and Grow Rich". It was first published in 1937. It was based on his studies of highly successful men and women. Such individuals as Henry Ford, George Eastman (Kodak), Theodore Roosevelt, Wilbur Wright, John D Rockefeller, Thomas Edison and many others. He distilled into 13 common principles, the reasons for their success.

These highly successful individuals' achievements were a result of their vision, their passion, their planning plus other principles which are no secret. The first and the last of the *Five Pillars of Guaranteed Business Success* have their roots in Napoleon Hill's formulation.

I think the secret to success was very well expressed by Dr Ivan Misner. He said:

> *The Secret of Success is the uncommon application of common knowledge.*

It is doing all the things we have discussed here, doing it in a highly disciplined manner and doing it very well.

The secret to success without hard work is a secret yet to be revealed and if someone has found it, they are keeping very quiet about it. (Wouldn't you!)

So the question for you today, is are you going to continue to search for the 'Silver Bullet' and continue the Business Opportunity Three-Step, are you going to rely on luck, and buy a lottery ticket — unfortunately the favourite wealth creation strategy for most the population, or are you going to roll up your sleeves and start doing what you know you have to do to be successful?

> *Opportunity is missed by most people because it is dressed in overalls and looks like work.* —Thomas Edison

You know the definition of insanity is doing the same thing over and over again, and expecting something different to happen.

What's Your Plan?

Chapter 12

Taking Action

The Eagle gently coaxed her offspring toward the edge of the nest. Her heart quivered with conflicting emotions as she felt their resistance to her persistent nudging. "Why does the thrill of soaring have to begin with the fear of falling?" she thought. This ageless question was still unanswered for her.

As in the tradition of the species, the nest was located high on the shelf of a sheer rock face. Below there was nothing but air to support the wings of each child. "Is it possible that this time it will not work?" she thought. Despite her fears, the eagle knew it was time. Her parental mission was all but complete. There remained one final task – the push.

The eagle drew courage from an innate wisdom. Until her children discovered their wings, there was no purpose for their lives. Until they learned how to soar, they would fail to understand the privilege it was to have been born an eagle. The push was the greatest gift she had to offer. It was her supreme act of love. And so one by one she pushed them, and they flew!

"Even Eagles Need A Push" by David McNally www.davidmcnally.com

This was how I started my business. I had a mentor who was supporting my early steps. He helped me in the initial mechanics. He gave me some training. Then he gave me 'The Push'.

"OK, Greg" he said, "I think you are ready". But I knew I wasn't. He said, "On Monday, I want you to execute the plan, and start making the calls". These were cold calls. I had no network, having just returned from working overseas for seven years. I wanted to argue with him that I needed more preparation, but I knew he was right. I could have spent one, two, three more weeks preparing, and it would still come to this point.

The real question was not whether I was ready, but:

How much did I want to have my own business?

The answer to that question was— I really wanted it. I saw it as an important personal development. I wanted to prove to myself that I could make this journey. I wanted it much more than avoiding the possibility of being not totally in control of a situation I knew was impossible to control. More preparation was not going to be as great a value as actually jumping into the market place.

You can never learn to drive a car from the passenger's seat.

So that is what I did. I jumped. Was it easy? No. Was it harder than I imagined? Yes. Would I do it the same way again? Yes.

For some, 'The Push' may come from their own internal determination. For others, the 'fear of flying' is so huge that they need help in understanding their motivations before they will respond to 'The Push'. In my case I was focused on looking at my street directory when my mentor, pointed out that the lights were green, and there were no obstacles in my path. I was ready.

I very much thank my mentor, Phil, for 'The Push'.

What I learned when I jumped were things no amount of reading, training or coaching could have provided, but my education did not end there. I became teachable. I was ready to listen, absorb, and act on the advice of others. I started to learn, what it was I did not know.

How much do you want your business to be a success? Have you determined the price you will pay? If you have, there is only one more question.

So when do You want to start? If your answer to this question is not right now, you are not serious about your goals. Some say they are not ready. This is the road to procrastination. You will never be ready. There will always be a reason to delay and always an opportunity cost that goes with it. It is more important to get it done than get it right. It does not have to be perfect the first time. If perfection was the secret of business success, we would still be waiting for Bill Gates to release Windows Version 1.0!

"No Plan Survives Contact with the Enemy" — Dwight Eisenhower

You can over plan. That does not mean you should not prepare contingencies, but it is never possible to exactly predict your market. You can only, engage, measure, and adjust, but until you engage, you will never know what you need to adjust.

At this point, you have:

- A goal about which you are passionate
- A goal for which you know the obstacles
- A goal for which you will make sacrifices to overcome these obstacles

The lights are green and there are no obstacles in your path that you can't overcome. You are ready to start now!

Action Steps

12.1 Tomorrow morning I will take the following steps to my future success:

_____

_____

_____

_____

_____

_____

12.2 At the end of this week I will have achieved:

_____

_____

_____

12.3 At the end of this month I will have achieved:

_____

_____

_____

_____

12.4 At the end of this quarter I will have achieved:

_____

_____

_____

_____

_____

12.5 At the end of this year I will have achieved:

_____

_____

_____

_____

_____

12.6 The key benefits to me when I achieve these goals are:

_____

_____

_____

_____

_____

12.7 The Key Obstacles to my success are:

_____

_____

_____

_____

12.8 My strategies to overcome these obstacles are:
(The Price I am willing to Pay)

_____

_____

_____

12.9 The name of someone to hold me accountable to this plan:

_____

12.10 I, _____ (insert your name),

do hereby commit to this plan.

Signature: _____ (Your Signature)

Witness: _____

(Signature of Person named in 12.9)

Dated: _____

Opportunities multiply as they are seized — Sun Tzu

RESOURCES

The following Tools and Resources can be obtained at no charge to purchasers of this book by visiting the website below:

Business Goals Generator Tool
Use this tool to help you define your vision and set goals.

Business Plan Template
This template is a step-by-step process for creating your Business Plan.

Profit Driver Calculator
This tool will enable you to set profit targets for your business and will help identify where your opportunities for profit growth lie.

Price — Profit Calculator
Use this tool to determine how much you should lift your prices.

Visit: www.pillarstools.FivePillarsBusinessSuccess.com

and enter your Name and Email, and the code: MyBusinessSuccess

I wish you every success as you implement the Five Pillars. Please send me your success stories and let me know how this book has helped your business by sending your comments to:

enquiry@GregChapman.biz

INDEX

About the Author

Dr Greg Chapman is a leading advisor of Emerging Businesses. He is a professional speaker, internationally recognised author, publisher and a business and marketing coach. Throughout his 25 years of business experience in seven countries, including eight years in the US and UK he has become knowledgeable on international best practice in business.

Dr. Chapman has been responsible for the operation of businesses and projects ranging from the micro to the billion dollar size. He lives and breathes a wide range of business solutions "from experience".

Through his company, Empower Business Solutions which provides business coaching and advice, and the Small Business Achiever – Business Owner Brief, Dr. Chapman is dedicated to assisting business owners with the 'Right Kind of Help.' He has created the Small Business Achiever in response to the demand by those who want access to his knowledge in bite-sized chunks.

As a result of his direct knowledge and experience in running businesses, Greg's approach is not like that of an accountant, a sales person, or a bank manager. He thinks and acts like a business owner. The advice he gives is based on his own knowledge — not from a manual written by someone else. So he is able to tailor his programs for the needs of individual business owners.

Greg also provides business education through seminars for professional organisations, large businesses seeking to connect to small businesses as well as courses at business schools at universities. He has a PhD from Melbourne University a MBA from Deakin University and is a Certified Master Coach from the Behavioral Coaching Institute. He is a member of the International Coaching Council and the Australian Institute of Company Directors. Greg is a judge for the Marketing & Communications Executives International Awards.

Find out more about Dr Greg Chapman at:

www.GregChapman.biz

and find out about the Small Business Achiever – Business Owner Brief at:

www.SmallBusinessAchiever.biz

www.ingramcontent.com/pod-product-compliance
Lightning Source LLC
Chambersburg PA
CBHW062020200326
41519CB00017B/4855